I0135404

little book of

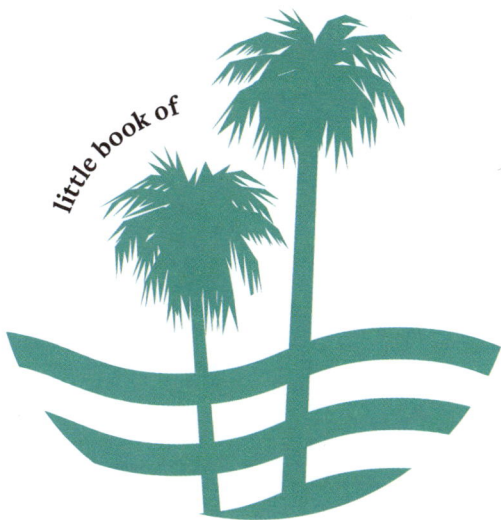

CALiFORNiA
style

Copyright © 2026 Headline Publishing Group Limited

First published in 2026 by Welbeck
An Imprint of HEADLINE PUBLISHING GROUP LIMITED

1

Apart from any use permitted under UK copyright law, this
publication may only be reproduced, stored, or transmitted, in
any form, or by any means, with prior permission in writing of the
publishers or, in the case of reprographic production, in accordance
with the terms of licences issued by the Copyright Licensing Agency.

Cataloguing in Publication Data is available from the British Library

ISBN 9781035433056

Printed and bound in Dubai

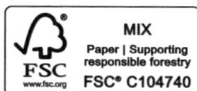

MIX
Paper | Supporting
responsible forestry
FSC® C104740

FSC
www.fsc.org

Headline's policy is to use papers that are natural, renewable and
recyclable products and made from wood grown in well-managed
forests and other controlled sources. The logging and manufacturing
processes are expected to conform to the environmental regulations
of the country of origin.

HEADLINE PUBLISHING GROUP LIMITED
An Hachette UK Company
Carmelite House
50 Victoria Embankment
London EC4Y 0DZ

The authorised representative in the EEA is Hachette Ireland,
8 Castlecourt Centre, Dublin 15, D15 XTP3, Ireland
(email: info@hbgi.ie)

www.headline.co.uk
www.hachette.co.uk

DEIRDRE CLEMENTE

little book of

CALIFORNIA
style

WELBECK

CONTENTS

introduction page 6

chapter 1:

THE BEACH

36

chapter 2:

MOUNTAINS

60

chapter 3:
DESERT
82

chapter 4:
HiGHWAY
108

chapter 5:
EPiLOGUE
138

index page 158
credits page 160

INTRODUCTION

From the sands of San Diego to the record shops of San Francisco's Haight-Ashbury, California style is born of place. A varied landscape where snow-capped mountains melt into green valleys and spiked cacti burst with fuchsia flowers, California also has more than three thousand miles of coastline.

Places and people make fashion: leg-warmer-ed Valley Girls; aspiring rappers in black sweatshirts and Oakland Raiders baseball caps; ranchers in beat-up jean jackets; golden-haired, flip-flopped surfers; Mexican-American women in the Chola style with flannel shirts buttoned at the neck, dark lipstick and hoop earrings; aspiring starlets in skimpy dresses. California *is* the cliché, and it has defined modern fashion. This book celebrates the state's most innovative and enduring contributions to our wardrobes and tells the story of how they got there.

Home to more than one hundred and fifty Indigenous tribes, California has abundant natural resources that have fuelled economic and cultural exchange since time immemorial as the Chumash (the "seashell people") established trade routes deep into the Southwest and the Karuk fished for salmon in the Klamath River with twelve-foot dip nets. California's abundance has attracted swathes of people looking for gold, or fame, or freedom. In 1939, a fashion editor mused, "No word is as richly burdened with connotations, glamour, romance, color, enchantment in the minds of the rest of the population as this: California."[1]

In this *GQ* 1972 fall fashion feature, San Francisco manufacturers celebrated their city. Featured here, a Western shirt from Jizz and A-1 Kotzin Pants, whose tag proclaimed "NO IRON". The lumberjack shirt remains a perennial favourite.

Free from East Coast rules about white shoes after Labor
Day, California made clothing for the West Coast way of
life. "The Westerner has the daring to wear what was made
for him when it fitted his mode of living," explained *Fortune*
magazine in 1945. This included "clothes for gardens and
beaches and sun-drenched city streets anywhere."[2] One-piece
rompers in colourful, printed rayon were great for bike rides.
The "lumberjack" shirt's name betrays its origins, as do board
shorts. Golf courses and tennis courts gave our wardrobes
sneakers, sport shirts, sweat suits, skorts, cardigans and
culottes – the wide-legged, knee-length shorts that live
peacefully between a skirt and pants. With its own sartorial
standards, California was a place where surfers could share
their swimwear and skateboarders their shoes with people
who never tried the sport. "Practical" trumped "appropriate"
in California.

Above: Surfing in California remained largely a practice for white men, with little celebration of the sport's roots in the Pacific Islands. As the century progressed, more women and people of colour began to participate.

Opposite: California supplied its growing population with produce, dairy and meat. From oranges to almonds, companies advertised the abundance of the land. This model wears a sleeveless blouse and vaguely "ethnic" skirt.

Above: Addie Masters made "patio clothes" designed to move seamlessly from the kitchen to the dining room to the poolside. Seen here in a 1954 spread in *Vogue* magazine, a sleeveless, blue linen dress is photographed in a home designed by architect Henry L. Eggers.

Opposite: Beloved by young women, two-piece sun ensembles and rompers were comfortable, washable, and sometimes controversial.

Sportswear

California style is built on sportswear. In its early years, women designers dominated the field: Bonnie Cashin, Viola Dimmitt, Louella Ballerino (one of her designs shown below left), Addie Masters, Tina Leser and Irene Bury. Designer-owned firms produced garments in-house to ensure high quality – a hallmark of the industry. Women innovated.

The widow of an Arizona rancher, Marjorie Montgomery built a successful firm on the popularity of her high-waisted pants in faded denim, a treatment process she pioneered in the 1930s. Sportswear designers came with practical knowledge. Once head of physical education at Whittier High School, Elizabeth Russell Myers had a Masters in mathematics from Stanford, which helped with the precise cut for her walking shorts and cropped jackets.

California style thrives on innovation. Manufacturers pioneered alternative sizes, including cuts for tall and fuller figures. They were widely responsible for the popularization of junior sizes that catered to younger women with smaller torsos. As opposed to New York or Chicago, manufacturers in Los Angeles and San Francisco didn't begin by forecasting their seasonal offerings months in advance. California's climate and comfort-driven culture lacked the rigid categories that regulated garments to a particular season or social event.

Since their inception in the mid-1910s, Los Angeles's manufacturers focused on small runs of trendy garments to see what sold, and then make more. Unlike other cities with complicated systems of subcontracting, California firms actually made the clothes they sold, ensuring quality and on-time delivery. Joseph Zukin dominated the casual dress market with a three-storey factory in downtown Los Angeles and four hundred employees. He believed his colleagues were "more alert" and "more eager" than those in New York and Paris, with their "traditions and inhibitions". In California, "We are forward looking. Our past is so recent it cannot teach us much."[3]

The twentieth century was the century of California. The rest of the country, and the world, first learned about it through travel writing by conservationist John Muir, Levi's advertisements and the short stories featuring Hopalong Cassidy. Clothing was central to California's image and way of life – cowboy hats to ward off the sun and rain; lounging pajamas for poolside cocktails; loose-fitting khakis for all that

San Francisco's Chinese-American designers merged the colours and motifs of their culture with the sensibility of California fashion. Seen here, slits on skirts allowed for fit and mobility.

driving. Visitors came and "bought liberally". They carried California-made garments back home and wore them there. In 1922, an insider confirmed "the real reputation that we have secured is accounted for by a prominent element – the tourist."[4] In 1927, Southern California welcomed two million visitors. Fifty years later, nine million yearly visitors spent $1.5 billion in the region.[5]

Many permanently relocated. California began the twentieth century with fewer than two million residents. In 2000, it was the fifth largest economy in the world with thirty-four million residents. Californians have long been racially and ethnically diverse. Black families took the train west to get out of the racist South. In 1920, around sixteen thousand Black people lived in Los Angeles. In 1930, there were forty thousand, a number that nearly doubled again by 1940 when it became the largest Black population of any western US city. Chinese labourers laid railroad tracks through the Sierra Nevada mountains and worked for a third of what their white colleagues received. German Jews fled the Nazis to Los Angeles, where they made up roughly 20 per cent of the population by the late 1950s. Indigenous people are both members of their tribal nation and citizens of California. Many tribes transcended government-imposed state boundaries and were diverse within themselves. The Pomo people in the North share common lineage and an expertise in basket making, but vary in language. The Tongva in the South built patterns of resistance to Spanish colonizers and their oppressive mission system that forced adults into labour and children into government-sanctioned boarding schools. Today, California has a strong and enduring presence of Indigenous people.

In many urban neighbourhoods such as West Oakland and Los Angeles's Watts and the upscale Baldwin Hills, Black women frequented a thriving network of private dressmakers. They commissioned custom-made "slacks" to wear on picnics, afternoon walks and backyard parties.

With its hand-tooled leather goods, vibrant floral embroidery, and bright colours, Mexico looms large in California style. Immigrants from Mexico and those of Mexican descent remained a consistent quarter of the state's population throughout the twentieth century. Farmers, ranch hands, seamstresses and domestic workers often passed between the two countries. Between 1942 and 1964, a successful labour recruitment initiative known as the

Introduction

Mexican-Americans brought a flair for the dramatic and an appreciation for tailoring to California style. The platform sandals seen here play to a long-standing tradition in Southern California.

Manufacturers brazenly commercialized traditional Mexican
handcrafts such as brightly coloured embroidery and white lacework,
as seen here in this promotional image from the late 1930s.

Bracero Program brought five million agricultural workers
into the country, mainly to California. Mexico's influence
fed the cultural and commercial success of Western wear. As
with symbols from Indigenous art such as the thunderbird,
clothing firms appropriated Mexican motifs with no regard
for original context. The "Western saddle stitch" used on
saddles and sandals alike was a direct borrow from Mexican
cowboys (*vaqueros*), whose influence on Western wear
cannot be overstated.

Introduction

when the lure
of California brings
you westward

— *a welcome*

Above: This government-made image documents the relocation and internment of Japanese Americans during the Second World War. Those with skills made clothing for other "evacuees." In the industry at large, 75 per cent of seamstresses were Mexican or of Mexican descent.

Opposite: Using mailing lists of women's clubs, I. Magnin sent postcards such as this one from the mid-1920s to potential tourists on the East Coast. The front copy reads, "When the lure of California brings you westward." The interior says, "A welcome and a service await you in the shops of I. Magnin & Co." The store's offerings, the card explains, "can nicely relieve you of all thoughts of clothes-preparedness until your arrival in California."

Introduction

Latina labour

Latina women were foundational to the California fashion industry and represent a consistent 75 per cent of the labour force throughout the twentieth century.

Their presence was first noticed in October 1933, when more than two thousand garment workers took to the streets of downtown Los Angeles. They protested being cheated on overtime and dismissed in downturns – a painfully common practice. Most were of Mexican origin and are identified on the historical record as "Spanish-speaking". This three-week protest did little to improve conditions, but changed the opinions of union leaders who had argued against their inclusion in the labour movement because of an "inability" to organize and act collectively.

Today, Latinas work alongside Korean women and still make up the majority of seamstresses in Los Angeles. Shop owners still violate labour laws, and workers still have little recourse. As with the 1933 strikers, many are undocumented. Whether making petticoats in east London in the 1880s or yoga pants in Guangzhou in the 2020s, the garment industry is built upon the exploited labour of women.

In 1932, women working in the Los Angeles garment industry averaged $22 a week and usually worked 40 weeks a year.

This charming 1940 sketch by designer James Galanos uses black ink to accent the silhouette and features his note, "Very Nice for Cruise." Galanos became the couturier of choice for First Lady of California and the United States Nancy Reagan.

Population growth drove a powerful industry. Garment making thrived in the dank sweatshops of San Francisco's Chinatown, where "entire families of three generations engaged in making garments." There, "in these holes unfit for human occupancy," "garments were made by the thousands."[6] The city's well-capitalized firms, such as Koret, Byer and the gargantuan Levi Strauss, had the means to build sunlit factories. Up and down the coast, knitting mills pushed out golf sweaters, athletic uniforms and the state's beloved swimwear. Downtown Los Angeles was the heart of the industry. Here, fourteen-storey lofts had retail on the ground floor, offices on the second, and then storeys of open space configured to the occupant's needs.

By the start of the Second World War, California's sportswear makers gave New York City competition in influence, if not volume. An enthusiast in 1945 touted the increasing "national demand for the tangible and intangible something that is symbolized by the California label". [7] The war united West Coast manufacturers, workers and retailers as they suffered through L-85, a government-issued restriction on fabric that forbade cuffs, double breasting, pleats and ruffles. Partnering with the federal government, Tabak of California converted 80 per cent of its facilities to make uniforms. Cole of California made parachutes by day and some swimsuits on the off-shift.

As wartime cooperation turned to post-war competition, the garment biz became the fashion industry. Father-son operations gave way to corporations that oversaw multiple labels in various markets. A reporter for the financial publication *Barron's* wrote of "a new look in the industry, particularly since World War II" that came "in contrast with early regional and even local styles". National corporations orchestrated the production of fashion. Now, "the same dress will sell equally well in Boston, Atlanta, San Diego or Honolulu." Everyone was buying more. Between 1947 and 1970, consumer spending more than quadrupled.[8]

In munitions and machinery factories, women worked under the direction of men. Pants became a required garment. Women did not give them up after the war.

Hollywood was a blessing and a curse for the state's fashion industry. Early on, the two vied for the same design talent, fabric supplies and workers, in an already tight labour market. Both came to realize that they were strongest when they worked together. Whether 1920s *Photoplay* or 1990s *InStyle*, glossy magazine layouts of celebrities posing poolside in California-made garments provided incalculable free publicity. Local manufacturers willingly provided their latest lines to television shows for the "extras". International blockbusters such as *Back to the Future* (1985) brought LA-based Guess? Jeans stonewashed jackets to the vanguard of youth fashion.

Hollywood vehicles such as *Back to the Future* (1985) brought Los Angeles-based brands into the international spotlight, as seen with Marty McFly's much-coveted, two-toned denim jacket by Guess? Jeans.

Above: Contrasting colours, dramatic draping, and intricate seaming defined Adrian's work for Joan Crawford, including this promotion image for *Grand Hotel* (1932).

Opposite: With hundreds of films for MGM and a slew of private clients, Adrian is best remembered for the ruby slippers and gingham dress he designed for Judy Garland in *The Wizard of Oz* (1939).

Adrian

Everyone paid attention when Hollywood's star costume designer Adrian opened a Beverly Hills salon in 1942. Having achieved national notoriety for his work on more than two hundred films, including *The Wizard of Oz* (1939), Adrian was the first costumer to successfully crossover into commercial fashion. The salon featured imposing white columns and a raised, round platform where models paraded. Success prompted in-store boutiques at elite retailers across the country. By 1952, Adrian had twenty-seven branch shops.

To the American public, Adrian was married to actress Janet Gaynor, but it was a "lavender marriage". Adrian was well known to be gay. Travis Banton, who worked with stars Clara Bow and Marlene Dietrich, had a similar arrangement. Their colleagues Howard Greer and Orry-Kelly were also gay, as were many from the next generation of couture-level commercial and costume designers, including James Galanos, Michael Novarese, Bob Mackie and his partner Ray Aghayan.

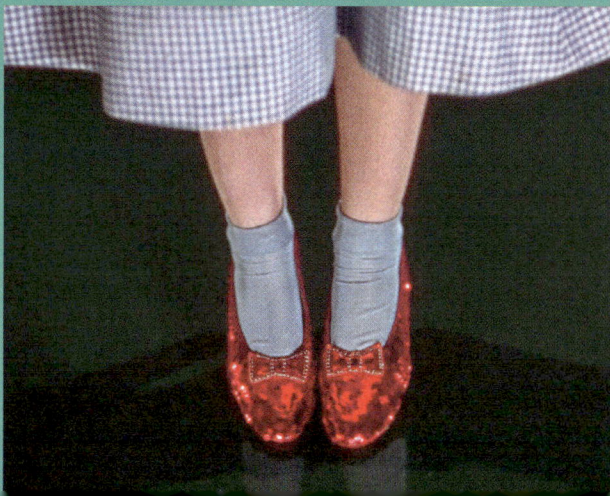

By the 1980s, the world understood California style through movies such as *Fast Times at Ridgemont High* (1982), *Beverly Hills Cop* (1984), *Bill & Ted's Excellent Adventure* (1989), *Pretty Woman* (1990) and *Clueless* (1995). The TV series *Beverly Hills, 90210* made what had been a horse trail into a household name. *The Fresh Prince of Bel Air* brought Black-owned, Southern California-based brand Cross Colours to international attention.

California style has two defining characteristics: it is born of place and it is versatile. This book celebrates locations for changing styles – the beach, the highway, the mountains and the desert. The geography itself set the demand, and clothes were made to accommodate the fact that within "an hour's time there is desert, ocean, and snow-capped mountains". *Women's Wear Daily,* which opened an office in Los Angeles in 1924, explained that California sportswear was the product of "a colorful, carefree country, where everyone plays as much as he or she can and wears comfortable clothes to do it".[9]

Versatility comes from the objects themselves. Featured here are the garments and accessories we use to craft our own California style – cowboy boots, pedal pushers, flip-flops and jeans. Much like the state itself, the power of California style is its diversity. While the rest of the world was slowly stepping away from the "when" and "where" rules of established fashion, Californians were already blurring the boundaries between formal and informal. California style mixes and matches seemingly incongruous garments: a breezy floral dress with a denim work shirt; gold chains and a baseball hat; a turquoise bolo tie with a tuxedo. Versatility comes from creativity and a willingness to flout convention – two things that Californians have in abundance.

Will Smith's bright wardrobe in *The Fresh Prince of Bel Air* brought Black-owned brand Cross Colours to screens around the world.

Clueless (1995) cemented the idea of LA high school style – from the matchy-matchy plaid suits to the white Calvin Klein slip dress, Cher Horowitz's wardrobe (sourced by costume designer Mona May) was preppy, grungey, slinky and naïve all at once.

Introduction

Above: Legendary designer Bob Mackie (centre) poses with Elton John, Flip Wilson, Bette Midler and Cher, who are all wearing his creations for the first episode of Cher's variety show in 1975.

Opposite: Body-building culture thrived in Southern California. Much like 1940s swimwear, elasticized fibres drove the design. Here, Cory Everson, six-time winner of Ms. Olympia, poses with another symbol of the state, the surfboard.

chapter 1

THE
BEACH

"If Clancy doesn't take me to the beach soon, I'll expire!" Marjorie Cherry wrote to her mother from her sorority house at Pomona College in 1929. She was desperate to wear new bell-bottomed beach pants that were "just the right size and color" and made her "feel Catalina-ish".[1] The next weekend, Clancy did take Marjorie to Catalina Island off the coast of Los Angeles, where she dropped chocolate ice cream down the front of them.

California style celebrates beach life and its required wardrobe: sunglasses, drawstring pants, bucket hats, cut-off jean shorts, flip-flops and tote bags. California dominated the early design and production of swimwear – a genre of dress that did not even exist a century before. Revolutions in recreation, technology, body consciousness and sexual mores cleared the way for the garment's transition from the East Coast's "bathing costume" to the West Coast's swimsuit. By 1960, the state made 90 per cent of the country's swimsuits. Surfing culture brought California's sun-kissed curls and nylon board shorts to the country and the world. Much like skaters and snowboarders, surfers were left to balance their rejection of modern consumerism with the commercial appeal of their lifestyle.

On the East Coast, beach communities policed the length of women's swimwear. Until the early 1920s, many beaches required black cotton stockings to ensure modesty. On the West Coast, male and female beachgoers wore form-fitting cuts in bright colours made by homegrown knitting mills. In California, knitting was big business. Albion Mills had

The Beach

Ground zero for American innovation, California was home to a thriving aviation industry that supplied new kinds of plastic foam and fibreglass to be used to make cheaper, more buoyant surfboards. Brought to market by DuPont in the 1930s as a synthetic rubber to be used in machinery, Neoprene fit the bill for protective wetsuits.

national distribution for its athletic uniforms. Broadway Mills made long underwear for loggers up and down the coast. In 1937, the industry's trade magazine, *Knitted Outerwear Times*, stressed the "increasing extent the California manufacturers of knitted sportswear and beachwear have been penetrating the eastern market". The public was eager to participate, and manufacturers were "seeking the California Ballyhoo as an aid to their merchandising". Hollywood designers helped to set trends with their "energy and creative ability".[2] California swimwear sold.

Above: Los Angeles-based fashion designer L'Tanya models her creations with a friend in the early 1940s. Many Black people frequented the beaches around Santa Monica where the lack of restrictive codes allowed for a more diverse crowd.

Opposite: Nearly 70 per cent of Californians live in a county that borders the Pacific Ocean. Seen here, debutantes in 1936 display a range of beach fashions, including sailor-inspired pants, oversized sun hats and sandals.

The Beach

Beach pajamas

Beach pajamas mark the first time that women wore pants in public in the name of fashion. In the late 1920s, they were worn as cover-ups on beaches in Miami and the south of France, a well-established incubator for new styles. Both Gabrielle "Coco" Chanel and exiled Russian designer Mary Nowitzky made high-end versions in France.

California makers capitalized on the trend and quickly saturated the local market. They made the pajamas in cotton or the increasingly popular rayon, which was marketed as "artificial silk". Made of cotton linters or cellulose from wood pulp mixed with nasty chemicals, rayon was spun into fibres and then woven. The initial results were shoddy, but as chemists hit upon better processes, rayon gained popularity because of its ability to be printed in bold patterns. In late 1929, San Francisco fashion writer Frances Piaget boasted to the readers of her national syndicated column, "I told you so! The brilliant beach pajama is enjoyed 'hither and yon' where there are fashionables."[3]

Beach pajamas even made the rare transition to eveningwear. Made of silk and decorated with fancy buttons, beadwork or an embroidered neckline, women wore evening pajamas in hotel lounges, to house parties and even at nightclubs. A 1935 *New York Times* article noted that the pajamas made "the line between beach clothes and dress frocks almost indistinguishable".[4] Layouts in Hollywood magazines of starlets sitting poolside in the pajamas gave the trend national traction that continued through the 1930s. These pajamas remain a chic "go-to" ensemble.

Beach pajamas came in different patterns and cuts, but their incredible popularity helped to introduce pants into women's wardrobes.

1930

DAVIDOW INC.

A 1958 advert for trailblazing California swimwear
company Catalina, featuring model Ann Klem.

The Beach

Southern California has long been a bastion for beachgoers. Officials at the Los Angeles Department of Playground and Recreation took their job seriously; their stationery bore the motto: "The test of whether a civilization will live or die is the way it spends its leisure." In the 1920s, they estimated that on a July weekend or summer holiday, more than half a million people headed to local beaches – a figure representing about 25 per cent of the county's population. From Pittsburgh to Portland, Americans were well aware of sunny California's coast from neighbours' postcards, books and magazines such as *Sunset*, which began as a promotional piece for the Southern Pacific Railroad and became the region's premier lifestyle publication.

Two powerhouse manufacturers bridged the gap between function and fashion in swimwear: Catalina and Cole of California. Founded in 1911, Pacific Knitting Mills changed its name to Catalina as a shout-out to the island, and focused on swimsuits in an array of sizes and styles. Its consistent corporate leadership built a network of department stores for national distribution and its tagline "Style for the Stars of Hollywood" reminded shoppers of its pedigree. Star designer Mary Anne DeWeese made trends and followed them. Her successful campaign for his-and-her matching suits was called "Sweethearts in Swimsuits". A former model, DeWeese catered to consumer demand, noting the always-increasing need for smaller, tighter suits. "If there is rubber in a bathing suit," she said, "buyers are hungry for it."[5] With her own firm, she specialized in custom suits for water skiers, outfitting entire teams on the national circuit. At the height of their power in the 1960s, Catalina owned twenty-two plants including a 175,000 square-foot, custom-built factory and offices in Los Angeles's garment district.

Sandals

California style requires the right shoes. Sandals have remained a staple of warm-weather wardrobes since the ancient Egyptians made them out of leather with soles of braided straw. California's mild climate allowed open-toed wedges, backless mules and woven, Mexican-inspired *huaraches* to be worn year-round.

In the early 1930s, technological advances in elastic fibres and the moulding of rubber pushed California footwear to the front of a national market for "play" shoes. Founded in 1929, Pasadena-based Joyce commanded the market. They made 150 pairs a day in 1931. Ten years later, they were up to 1,500 pairs and in 1946 they made 3,500 pairs. Fern Shoe Company started as a custom shop in 1919, transitioned to slippers, and then into street shoes and evening sandals. Following the Second World War, Fern sent the majority of the 3,000 pairs they made a day to the Midwest and East Coast. Like swimwear manufacturers, shoemakers had national distribution for products made and tested in California.

Flip-flops remain the most celebrated of California's sandals. Born as shower shoes in the 1940s, water-friendly flip-flops won praise in dormitory bathrooms and public pool dressing rooms. Inspired by the T-strap thongs of Japanese zōri, the rubber sandals moved into beachwear in the 1960s and mainstream production in 1974, when Rainbow Sandals started making them commercially, soon followed by Deckers and eventually Reef Shoes, founded in La Jolla in 1984.

Marketing their foam soles and colourways with vigour. The sandal manufacturer Joyce was one of 44 firms in the state that collectively made more than 15,000 pairs a day.

joyce
(CALIFORNIA)

The sun *must* shine this summer! Let it shine on you in your joyce sandals. Wear them on the beach, by the river, for holidays, picnics, week-ends, any time there's casual fun afoot. They're fashioned with friendly joyce comfort and drenched in sparkling joyce colours — the most lovable, intriguing sandals you ever lost your heart to.

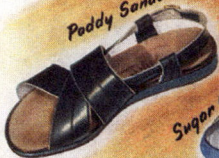

Paddy Sandal

Cat's Cradle

Sugar Cane

Sundial

Mexicoolee

Write for details of latest joyces to JOYCE (CALIFORNIA) LTD. Dept. G.H.2. 37-38 OLD BOND STREET, LONDON, W.I. Wholesale only.

The founder of Cole of California was a man born in the right place at the right time. Fred Cole's parents owned West Coast Manchester Knitting Mills at the dawn of Hollywood, and he worked as a silent screen actor before getting into the family business.

In 1936, he hired dancer-turned-designer Margit Fellegi whose forty-year tenure produced the most recognizable swimwear styles in history, including the Swoon Suit – a wartime, rubber-free, two-piece suit with lace-up bottoms and a bandeau top. Cole took California style international. He licensed its name to manufacturers around the world. His daughter, Anne, later took the helm with resounding success. "We'd all like to live as exciting of lives as our bathing suits live – jetting to the Riviera, Mexico and all over," she told the fashion press in 1976.[6]

Across the country, people wore swimsuits from Catalina and Cole of California to pools, beaches, lakes and backyard sprinkler parties. Smaller firms innovated. In the 1930s, Mabs Barnes, a retired dancer and founder of Mabs of Hollywood, wove cotton and the elastic fibre Lastex into a fabric that editors raved "gives stretch and control where they are most needed, resulting in flattering, functional suits".[7] First used to make surgical supplies, Lastex transitioned to foundation garments, then swimwear. Fred Cole created his own version called Mabletex to avoid paying the middle man. Sold at the popular Bullock's department stores, Mabs's suits were known for their interior construction and waist-cinching abilities. They were seen in movies, magazines and on stars such as Joan Crawford and Jean Harlow.

Swimsuits from top designers Mabs of Hollywood, Caltex, Cole of California and Catalina are seen here in a photoshoot for *Vogue* in 1949.

Above: Both men and women got tighter, faster drying swimsuits with Lastex, an elasticized fibre with a rubber core that is wrapped in layers of cotton or rayon. Launched in 1931 by the United States Rubber Company, Lastex can be made thicker or thinner, tighter or looser according to application.

Opposite: Costumer Adrian takes inspiration from the beach and Surrealist artists in this two-piece dress that features a hand-painted aquatic design, c.1944. The pattern is uninterrupted thanks to clever seaming, a signature of the master.

Above: Japanese-American beauty pageant contestants
stick with conservative styles in 1941.

Overleaf: Surf movies celebrated wholesome fun. Director William
Asher explained that his genre-defining film *Beach Party* (1963) was
about "kids having a good time and not getting in trouble".[11]

Rose Marie Reid also innovated to distinguish herself in an ever-growing market. A former gymnast and devout Mormon, Reid carefully placed elastic bands on the straps, legs and bust of her suits to ensure a better fit on a wider range of bodies. A lifelong sewer, she got major distribution when Lord & Taylor's merchandise buyer saw the hourglass-shaped suits in her hotel room – a visit the designer considered "the hand of God".[8] Reid did not cater to movie stars but to regular shoppers, including larger-framed women, a neglected market. In 1950, Reid went on a national tour to retailers where she gave out pamphlets entitled, "You yes, you!" and engaged with shoppers and staff. "I'm crusading to teach sales-girls how to fit swimsuits," she told the *Idaho Daily Statesman*.[9] Reid designed suits for stout women, tall women and pear-shaped women. Reid was constantly under pressure to put out bikinis – a design that did not sit well with her Mormon beliefs.

In 1960, California was the most populous state in the country, and its beach life had an international presence. The popular *Gidget* books that followed the adventures of a girl surfer were quickly made into a movie in 1959 and a television series. In contrast to juvenile delinquents in hot rods, surf movies such as *Muscle Beach Party* (1964) and *How to Stuff a Wild Bikini* (1965) offered a wholesome and hodgepodge interpretation of surf life. A scholar called the film genre a celebration of "nonconformist, irreverent, and anti-bourgeois attitudes" that were "cobbled together from elements of teenage culture, rock-and-roll, bohemian philosophy, and beat culture" and then "mixed with a healthy dose of parody".[10] Only one member of the music group the Beach Boys actually surfed, but they all sang about it. California's surf culture was lucrative.

The commodification of surf culture brought opportunities for some but was met with disdain from others. Despite the sport's Polynesian origins, surfing remained a white person's sport for decades. In Southern California, many beaches were segregated because of racist policies by private landowners and city officials. Additionally, urban development projects such as highways and trainlines further separated mixed-race neighbourhoods from natural resources. Surf movies celebrated a white-bread version of California that denied its racial and ethnic diversity.

As with ski resorts and tennis clubs, California's beaches each developed their own distinct surf culture with social hierarchies and wardrobe preferences. The communities south of Los Angeles, including El Segundo, Manhattan Beach, Redondo Beach and Torrance, hosted international surf competitions sponsored by homegrown brands such as wetsuit pioneer Body Glove and Ocean Pacific, which transitioned from boards to clothing in the late 1970s. Their thigh-skimming corduroy shorts in bright colours remain a definitive trend of the early 1980s. Authenticity remained paramount to the success of surf brands. Team sponsorship maintained a brand's connection to the culture.

The Beach

The Beach Boys were marketed as the quintessential, fun-loving California boys, complete with beach-friendly chinos and lumberjack shirts from Pendleton. The Oregon-based woollen mills occupy a prime place in the history of West Coast fashion, having supplied wool for many of the blankets produced by Indigenous tribes for their own ceremonies and commercial sales.

Board shorts

Board shorts came from necessity. Regular swimsuits were too short to protect surfers' legs from rashes and their tight seams popped during the action. Hang Ten co-founder Duke Boyd invented a better garment. He remembered, "When I started Hang Ten, I was discharged from the service, living off the GI Bill. I knew nothing, except surfing." Boyd commissioned seamstress Doris Boeck to make the six samples of board shorts that quickly sold at a local surf shop. To attest to the brand's authenticity, they named it Hang Ten, after a difficult surf move in which the surfer's feet are together with all ten toes curled over the side of the board. By the end of the century, the business had $450 million in sales and an international reputation. *Women's Wear Daily* wrote, "The name Hang Ten conjures up images of beaches, surfers and true California style."[12]

Other surfer-led companies pushing board shorts included Katin and O'Neill, the Santa Cruz-based maker of neoprene body suits. Following demand, swimwear brand Catalina sent designer Maurice Levin to the beaches of Santa Monica for practical information. The surfers told him no zippers or buttons. For his Sunfari collection, Levin created "a surfer's belt" that tied in the front at the waist. Much of Levin's inspiration came from Southern California culture, where "the surfer look is always the hottest thing." Bill Williard, a high school sophomore in 1965, was an actual surfer and annoyed at the sport's newfound popularity; "Every guy from San Bernadino to Milwaukee can buy surfing trunks, they used to be custom made."[13]

To protect both the wearer and the board, designers turned to one of the oldest forms of closure for pants: the drawstring waistband.

chapter 2

MOUNTAINS

California style comes from the mountains. There, in the Sierra Nevada, the Cascades and the Klamath, California style acquired its utilitarian tenets – durability, warmth and weather resistance. In the logging towns of Mendocino and the alpine resorts of Big Bear, labourers and leisure-seekers learned to dress for the environment. The diversity of California's landscape confused and intrigued readers around the country. "What is true of one locality is not true of another," wrote Reverend E. Graham in an 1875 missive to a paper back in New York. Regardless, the weather was "no restraint from the freest exercise outside".[1]

The clothing worn and popularized in these mountains was the physical embodiment of practicality – flannel shirts, lumberjack coats, Shetland sweaters, leather boots and "drilling" pants, the progenitor of our beloved chinos. Distinctions of class that drove fashion in cosmopolitan places seemed irrelevant in the remote mining camps of La Porte and Gibsonville in the north-east of the state. There, miners organized ski races for prize money and experimented with the right formula for their wax – or, as they called it, "dope" – which was used to grease up their skis. Wardrobe frivolities were left to the tourists.

California's temperate climate allowed for creative interpretation of winter wear, as seen with these swimsuit-clad women on the slopes in 1941.

Mountains

The mountains of California have long been sites for social, cultural and economic change. With the influx of Easterners in the late nineteenth century, a rush for natural resources such as timber and gold ran congruently with a celebration of outdoor recreation. For both, clothing was consistently centre stage. An 1868 guidebook for Yosemite explained that visitors will be "very uncomfortable" if they don't adequately prepare: "both men and women need heavy, thick-soled, calf-skin boots, leather gloves, and stout dress of cheap material." "Every lady" needed "at least a pair of blue drilling pants" and a "bloomer dress" – a knee-length skirt worn over full trousers.

Durability comes from a cloth's weave. Used for raincoats and work pants, wool gabardine is a twill, tightly woven on the diagonal for sturdiness. By treating the wool before weaving, manufacturers achieved better weatherproofing. Chambray, by comparison, is a plain-weave in cotton or linen. Because it was lightweight and washed well, it was used for work shirts. Denim was similar but more tightly woven, making it heavier and more rigid. Flannel was a godsend for mountaingoers. Despite its French-derived name, flannel was first made in seventeenth-century Wales for farm workers. Its use of second-rate wool fibres made it warm and affordable. These fibres are softened by "carding" – a manual process that uses spiked paddles to align strands and comb out knots and dirt. Then, the wool is spun and woven as a plain weave or twill. After weaving, the cloth is rubbed (or "napped"),

Mountains

Oakland-born Bonnie Cashin is the grand dame of California sportswear. Best known for her creative use of materials and uncomplicated design, Cashin grew up in her mother's dress shop, began making costumes for dance troupes, and became an early advocate for lifestyle dressing. This wool and cashmere wrap speaks to her clothing's simple luxury.

dyed, and then rubbed again to "fluff" up the surface. In the United States, Detroit-based Carhartt milled its cloth in the South and dominated distribution of flannel shirts with production facilities around the country including in San Francisco.

Flannel became a calling card for California style. Old-school garment maker Brownstein Lewis made the state's first flannels in the late 1890s. These were woven in the now-classic, red-and-black checked "buffalo" pattern, known outside the US as Rob Roy tartan. Scottish textile makers marketed it as the tartan of the so-named folk hero. In the States, Woolrich Mills in central Pennsylvania made flannel in the buffalo pattern as early as the 1850s. With solid distribution, the shirt became a favourite of hunters, trappers and fisherman. The well-named "lumberjack" shirts and jackets popularized the pattern in California and became time-tested moneymakers.

Workwear seamlessly responded to the practical needs of outdoor life. As the adoption of the breast pocket with overlapping flap demonstrates, necessity was the mother of invention. Now seen on sports shirts, military uniforms and safari duds, this pocket was first used in California. In 1889, Cohn-Goldwater of Los Angeles made work clothes. The men making explosives for California Powder Works in Hercules did not wear coats and had nowhere to put their cigarettes. To meet demand, the company made a shirt with these pockets, and used them again in their popular short-sleeved golf shirt introduced in the mid-1910s.

This 1939 jumpsuit uses wool bouclé for a nubbly texture and durability. Images such as this from the *San Francisco Examiner* promoted locally made garments for the region's outdoor life.

Mountains

Campers began the century as a powerful demographic in California, a privileged position that continues today with home-grown mega brands Patagonia and The North Face. Early campers bought leather boots with corrugated soles, bib overalls, long underwear and knee-length socks. Laundry in camp was rough. An 1895 account describes a camping trip that took place where "a great dark mountain rose behind the spring" on the edge of a "valley, unfenced and dotted with browsing herds". There, women and children "put home-made soap on the clothes, dipped them in the spring, and rubbed them on the smooth rocks until they were white as snow".[2]

Cars made camping more convenient. The editors of *Outing* magazine trumpeted that campers were now "free to roam, to camp, and to change your ground at will, to surmount the obstacles of the open country".[3] Car camping spawned an entire industry of necessary equipment, such as Coleman stoves and coolers. These accoutrements, said *Sunset* magazine, made sure that campers had "more of the luxuries and niceties of home living".[4]

In 1953, Patagonia founder Yvon Chouinard began climbing in Southern California, and forged pitons for his friends for $1.50 each. Today, Patagonia is an international powerhouse that popularized the synthetic pile fleece jacket, a stalwart for outdoor enthusiasts and tech bros.

Mountain wardrobes required warm garments. Construction workers, hikers, snowshoers and alpine picnickers all learned from experience that "warm" did not necessarily mean "heavy". Knitwear – a genre of dress that included hosiery, athletic uniforms, swimwear, underwear and sweaters – gave consumers clothing that was both cozy and comfortable in a range of temperatures. Mechanized knitting frames had been used in England since the second half of the sixteenth century, and engineers advanced the technology with decades of trial and error. After the American Civil War, the nascent menswear industry pushed hard into new technology for all kinds of garment production. By the early 1900s, rotating cylinders pumped out sweater sleeves in under a minute. New kinds of needles created a finer gauge. Coupled with the introduction of elasticized fibres, delicate knits came along at a critical time when the East Coast's garters were being given up for the sports sock – a California-made favourite for men and women alike.

Knitwear was a cut-throat business in San Francisco, the state's main garment city for the first quarter of the twentieth century. Technology, know-how and styling could make or break a firm in a single season. The prolific J.J. Pfister Knitting Company mass-produced bathing suits, wool tights and sporting uniforms. They sold wholesale around the region and ran a custom shop in downtown for the local crowd. A decade into its success, the company's secretary and its mill superintendent took their accrued knowledge and founded Gantner & Mattern, later known as Gantner of California. Their "Wikie" model replaced the one-piece suits of the past.

Buying right from the supplier, the specialty boutiques of California ski towns sold regionally made garments, such as this sweater and matching headband.

As industry and tourism brought more people onto California's mountains, innovations in garment production and fibre science continuously pumped creative energy into its knitwear. Owner-run firms such as powerhouse Maurice Holman offered youthful designs and produced in small runs so they could adapt to emerging trends. This combination established the California knitwear industry as a leader in an increasingly national market.

"California manufacturers made a cornucopia of sweaters in an endless variety of cuts, patterns and sizes."

To satiate consumers' need for warmth and style, California manufacturers made a cornucopia of sweaters in an endless variety of cuts, patterns and sizes. Some were rough-hewn, such as the Shetland sweater, named after the Scottish islands, and which boasted a dense, nearly water-resistant wool. Some came as oversized cardigans, like the much-bemoaned "Sloppy Joe" of the late 1930s – a teenage craze that confused knitwear designers and irked mothers. Some sweaters featured collars and cuffs for a dressier look. Of the millions of sweaters made and worn in California, there is a special place for the home-made variety. In the summer of 1918, Agnes Edward spent much of her family's camping vacation making one. Back on campus that fall, she wrote to her mother, "I initiated my sweater today. It's just warm enough and such a pretty shade of blue. I like it so much."[5]

Mountains

Two brothers pose in San Francisco's Western Addition neighbourhood. One wears a red, custom-made knit suit from local tailor, Lili Knits.

Skiwear merged durability, warmth and weather resistance for a sport-specific genre of dress with mass appeal. In both construction and styling, skiwear owed much to the clothing of the Austrian and Swiss Alps where the sport originated. Norway's knitting traditions supplied patterns and notions such as metal frog-clasps. Many innovators were European, such as Bogner, a German brand that pioneered ski pants made from interwoven nylon and wool – a clever trick soon borrowed by California's makers. These snug-fitting pants invaded the slopes of Sugar Bowl near Lake Tahoe in the early 1950s, and were much talked about in the 1960 Winter Olympics in nearby Squaw Valley (now known as Palisades Tahoe) – the first time that organizers insisted that American firms made the official uniforms for the Games.

With a strong history of ski racing in northern mining camps and unlimited access to synthetic fibres, California manufacturers excelled in active skiwear. In the 1930s, the entire sport grew exponentially as ski trains took San Diegans from their rocky beaches just a few hours away to the slopes of Big Pine Park, home to a world-class ski jump. The rigours of the sport inspired designers and entrepreneurs to consciously reinvent. "Three or four years ago, when manufacturers first began placing ski togs, much of the merchandise was not right for active skiing," *Women's Wear Daily* reported in 1939. "These mistakes are gradually being corrected."[6] Much of the impetus came from the skiers themselves. Much like surf and skateboarding brands, many successful skiwear makers were founded and led by practitioners of the sport.

Mountains

California's Mammoth Mountain hosted competitive ski events with international racers such as Karen Korfanta. Ski sweaters gained warmth from wool that was woven with synthetic fibres to achieve bright hues in decorative stripes. Double-knit sweaters are two-ply garments that hug the body and can be made to be reversible.

Nylon came to be the main water-resistant fibre used in gauntlet gloves, boot gaiters, hooded jackets and pants. The first truly synthetic fibre, nylon met with rave reviews in the Second World War. In 1946, a top military brass told radio listeners, "Nylon comes closer to meeting ideal requirements for a great many uses of Army ground troops than any other fiber we have today."[7]

Activewear was a niche audience, but California's ski-inspired styles had broader appeal. Store windows featured après-ski jumpsuits with fur hoods, perfect for snuggling around a fire. Waterproof anoraks, stirrup-bottomed knitted leggings and fur earmuffs sold in seasonal shops of major department stores. On the East Coast, Bloomingdale's sold Tyrolian sweaters in its popular North Bound Shop and Wanamaker's Swiss Winter Village had yodellers and an eighty-foot ski slide. San Francisco's I. Magnin celebrated its selection of European designers working in the field, such as early birds Jean Patou and Elsa Schiaparelli, both of whom made one-piece snowsuits in the early 1930s. In the 1950s, I. Magnin's dozen stores carried sportswear pioneers Irene Galitzine and the maestro of knitwear Emilio Pucci, who began his career designing for the slopes of Cortina.

Demands for practicality fuelled innovation. On the chairlifts, in tents, by the stream and at the rock face, workers and sportspeople required garments that met their needs. California style delivered.

Paired with a matching jacket, nylon bib overalls became the ski pants of choice in the early 1970s.

Legendary costumer Edith Head designed this knit-jersey
ensemble, complete with palazzo pants, a roomy tunic, and
matching headband, perfect for après-ski socializing.

Not everyone had the chance to go skiing, so manufacturers offered alternatives. The market falls into three categories: activewear, ski-inspired styles and après-ski garments. California-made products dominated national and eventually, international sportswear.

Snowboard style

Excess gear from America's military conflicts flowed into California's surplus stores, such as Orange County's Rancho Army-Navy and Surplus City, an hour north of Sacramento. There, campers found collapsable frying pans, nylon rope and cargo pants. These government-issued cotton-twill trousers were standard-issue military uniforms in the Second World War. Campers were avid surplus scavengers, and took to the drawstring waist and patch pockets with front gussets for more space. Because the baggy pants allowed for leg mobility and, ironically, aligned with their anti-establishment ethos, skaters got on board in the 1980s. Then, came something new.

Thrill-seeking Californians fell in love with snowboarding in the early 1990s at resorts such as Soda Springs near Lake Tahoe, known as the state's "snowiest" place, with strong ski racing traditions and an epic halfpipe. The world came to know the sport through the X Games, an international competition of extreme sports first broadcast from Oceanside, California to nearly two hundred countries and in twenty-one languages. In the 2000s, Shaun White, a kid who had trained with skateboarding legend Tony Hawk in their hometown of San Diego, dominated the sport. White set the sport's fashion, pioneering snow "jeans" and known for his omnipresent knit skull cap.

Cargo pants needed creative interpretation for the slopes. Key points of contact such as knees and butts got reinforcement from extra fabric. More traditional skiwear manufacturers struggled to convince riders that their boards and garb could match the innovative styles of those made by pioneering practitioners such as California's Tom Sims. His namesake company operated under his own fashion motto,

Snowboarding, like skateboarding and surfing, was all about "authenticity". McDonald's, Mountain Dew, and Polo Sport clamoured for partnerships. Pioneers such as Vermont-based Burton and French skiwear giant Rossignolm sold the gear and the garb. Trend-savvy companies such as Kurvz Extremewear in Davis, California provided the masses with what they termed "snow apparel".

"If you can't be the best rider in the group, be the best-dressed." Pants manufacturers placed patch pockets on the diagonal to avoid snow accumulation and used heavy-duty plastic zippers to resist freezing. Stylistically, snowboarding gear was more brash than skiwear or skatewear. Neon hues, colour blocking and vibrant patterns got as much attention as one's riding.

chapter 3

DESERT

The Sonoran Desert teems with life. The 100,000 square-mile desert spans north-west Mexico and the south-west United States, and is home to nearly four hundred types of birds, one hundred kinds of reptiles and more than one thousand native bee species. The desert fan palm is the region's most distinct resident. The Cahuilla, the people of the Coachella Valley at the base of the San Jacinto mountains, believe the plant was a gift from the first man, Ma-ul. His desire to outlive mortality inspired him to stand at the base of a spring until his legs became bark and his hair became palm fronds. These fronds provided housing, clothing, shoes and cooking utensils for the Cahuilla people, whose trade routes spread the palm across the region.

In the desert, California style unites the utility of workwear with the embellishment of an invented American West. Dirty boots are worn with an embroidered cowboy shirt. California style also celebrates outdoor living. Tennis whites go from the court to a cocktail party with nary a glance. Whether worn by movie stars or maintenance men, jeans are central to life in the Californian desert. Jeans were first popularized at dude ranches, vacation destinations where visitors rode the range, fixed fences and ate baked beans from a can. There, as a 1941 sociological study put it, "millionaires, bankers, lawyers, artists, writers, school teachers, debutantes, dowagers, democrats and republicans mingle in carefree friendliness for a hilarious time."[1] San Francisco powerhouse Levi's leaned hard into advertising and education. At the promotional events they held in stores, they passed out pamphlets to tell the masses that jeans "are worn over the boot, not tucked into it".[2]

What the public came to view as Western wear was a creative interpretation of the real deal. California was home to extensive ranching and dairy farming. Real ranchers wore bandanas to protect their collars and rolled cowboy hats to funnel away rain.

It was another asset of the Cahuilla people that ended
up attracting outsiders to what is today Palm Springs – a
twelve-thousand-year-old underground mineral hot spring,
whose high pH and magnesium-rich properties reduce blood
pressure and relieve skin conditions. The Cahuilla set up
residence in palm-filled canyons in the summer and relocated
to their thatched-roof shelters near the springs in the winter.
In the 1860s, this water brought land developers looking
for a stopping point between Los Angeles and Prescott,
Arizona. With federal and state governments paving the
way, developers occupied the land, complicated access to
the springs for the Cahuilla, and spent a century building an
international reputation on the abundant natural resources
of the Sonoran Desert. The arrival of the stagecoach in the
area in 1862 brought a smallpox epidemic that devastated
the Indigenous people. In 1876, the Southern Pacific Railroad
carried in entrepreneurs, service workers, ranch hands and
new residents.

Palm Springs was a little desert town with a big cultural
footprint. Just one hundred miles east of Los Angeles, the
place has been a style centre since the dawn of Hollywood
in the 1910s. Its influence on American apparel is profound.
In 1937, a fashion editor remarked, "As goes Palm Springs, so
goes the nation."[3]

They called it "the desert season" – that time between
November and April when cooler temperatures make
sightseeing, sports and sun-soaking so much more enjoyable.
Health seekers found treatments for asthma and arthritis

These women pair wide-legged pants with their masks and
party hats. Their California-made footwear includes loafers
(worn with and without socks) and elastic sandals.

Desert

VIOLA S. DIMMITT
AND
BARNEY MAX present
A 'NEW' FIRM

"CASA CALIFORNIA"
SPORTSWEAR

LOS ANGELES

#717. Clam digger slack in Casha cloth.
$22⁵⁰ doz.

#718. Jacket in Western print.
$30⁰⁰ doz.

#720. Bra in Western print.
$15⁷⁵ doz.

(The hat is authentic 10 gallon.)

719 SO. LOS ANGELES ST.
LOS ANGELES, CALIF.

#703

#703 Linen Sunback Dress. Hand-blocked bolero. Bag and hat separate.
$4⁷⁵

#700. Celbrook Sharkskin Ensemble. Backless polka dot bra and sash. Hat separate.
$10⁷⁵

#708. Celbrook Sharkskin. One-piece dress with colorful belt and monogram.
$8⁷⁵

#700

in the healing waters and desert air. The famous Desert Inn and Sanitorium gave bottles of spring water as parting gifts. Nellie Coffman founded the facility with her husband in 1909, and turned the property into holy ground for American tourism and inspired the development of other desert destinations, such as Tucson and Santa Fe. Her motto: "Make Palm Springs attractive to attractive people." The Desert Inn had the town's first art gallery and pool. Retailer Bullock's kept a shop in its lobby and a full-fledged store a few blocks away. At its height in the 1940s, the resort employed two hundred workers from diverse racial and ethnic backgrounds to maintain its all-white amenities, including a large cactus garden and facilities for ping-pong, horseback riding, archery and star gazing. At his namesake piano bar, composer Jimmy Van Heusen sang 'Come Fly With Me' and other songs he wrote for Frank Sinatra, who had a house just up the road.

Palm Springs attracted film industry people, and that brought clout. Free of the "social register" feel of elite East Coast resorts, Palm Springs attracted all types: "lungers" looking to breathe easy in the desert air; California-curious Europeans with money to spend; wealthy families from across the Midwest passing through on their way to other well-curated tourist destinations such as Arrowhead Springs Hotel or Hotel Arcadia in Santa Monica. Palms Springs was popular. By the mid-twentieth century, it had more than three hundred hotels and half a million visitors a year. Its architecture still inspires pilgrimages and doctoral dissertations.

Clothing firms played to Western themes in their advertisements. This ad features culottes alongside a white dress and matching bolero jacket with Mexican-inspired embroidery. The firm Casa California was a collaboration between designers Barney Max and Viola Dimmitt.

Desert

With 350 days of sunshine a year, everyone came to sit poolside and admire each other's clothes. Industry advocate and *Los Angeles Times* fashion editor Sylva Weaver explained the enduring phenomenon in 1937: "Palm Springs vacationists are photographed, they are widely described, they are widely copied." In the end, "What they wear in the bright winter sun is what most of Mr. and Mrs. American will be wearing in the bright summer sun."[5] Weaver surveyed the landscape. Men wore short-sleeved button-up sports shirts with boat shoes. Women wore floppy sun hats, high-waisted frontier pants, two-piece swimsuits, and their tennis garb everywhere. A confluence of money, media attention, leisure and luxury came together to establish Palm Springs as a soothsayer of California style.

The Round Up fashion event of 1942 cemented this reputation. This three-day menswear extravaganza united manufacturers, retailers, famous golfers, B-list celebrities, fashion journalists and department store buyers. Sponsored by the Men's Apparel Guild in California (MAGIC), the Round Up offered marketing workshops and seminars on sales techniques. Each year, the Round Up grew. In 1947, 2,000 buyers came from thirty-two states and five countries. By 1955, it reached 2,500 buyers. United Airlines assigned a plane just to get people there. Nearly 3,000 people came to the event in 1960. Store buyers made decisions at the Round Up which reverberated in men's everyday wardrobes around the country and the world.

Fashion and architecture do more than co-exist in California. They integrate. In private homes and public spaces, the sleek simplicity of California modernism was experienced by all the senses. Architect Richard Neutra built the physical landscape – celebrating the state's greatest asset – into this Palm Springs property, as shown here in Slim Aarons' famous 1970 photograph *Poolside Gossip*.

Above: World-class embroidery firms such as Los Angeles's Viola Grae created desert-inspired designs, such as this desert rose design for cowboy film star Rex Bell. Husband to silent screen star Clara Bow, Bell sold his Walking Box Ranch brand at specialty stores throughout the West. Grae also worked for famed Western wear houses N. Turk and Rodeo Ben.

Opposite: This brightly hued, fringed shirt with mother-of-pearl snap closures pushes the boundaries of colour coordination, a signature of California style. Historian Cindy Aron writes that in the 1920s and 1930s, "Resorts themselves became sites of change – creating environments in which vacationers could also experiment with new, less restricted rules of conduct."[4]

Desert

The Round Up marked the beginning of a new era for menswear, one that would come to fruition in the coming decades. As merchandise buyers anticipated and interpreted shoppers' demands, an increasingly corporate fashion industry adjusted its business practices to accommodate a diversifying landscape of American men. These men bought clothing based on lifestyle rather than socio-economic status. Eventually, the Round Up went over the top. In 1957, MAGIC hired the producer of the Academy Awards to create a rotating stage on the enormous lawn of the Desert Inn. Nearly seventy models in clam diggers, "vest" shirts and itty-bitty swim shorts in leopard print took to the runway. Rebranded from the "Round Up" to simply "MAGIC" in the early 1960s, the event became the most important annual menswear trade show in the world and is now hosted in Las Vegas.

The Round Up exemplifies the paradoxical role that "Western wear" plays in California style. Elements of both the imagined and real American West can be seen in the aesthetic and function of a garment. It can be as blatant as embroidered cactus blooms along the hem of a broomstick skirt, or as subtle as the extra fabric on the shoulders of jean jacket, placed to prevent wear from carrying a saddle. A cornucopia of California-made options allowed shoppers from San Jose to Savannah to cherry-pick their own version of Western wear. Manufacturers rushed the Round Up's most popular items into production. At the 1942 inaugural event, a gabardine cowboy shirt with bright yellow bulls won the prize for best design. A lasso-inspired stitch decorated the collar, yoke and pockets. The fashion editor of the *San Francisco Chronicle* covered the buzz and reminded readers of the bigger "lesson learned" from the Round Up: "You don't have to have a ranch to wear a rancho sports jacket."[7]

The annual Round Up turned menswear into big money, growing from $8 million in garment sales in 1934 to $160 million just twenty years later, an increase of nearly 2000 per cent.[6]

Desert

Cowboy boots

Every feature of the cowboy boot is about function. The toe bed is narrow so it can slide into stirrups, and the stacked, angled heel is designed to keep it there. The calf-length leather body protects the shins and gives ankle support. Incarnations of the boot have had a recurring role in footwear since they were first used by the cavalry of ancient Assyria.

For American consumers, cowboy boots found a mass market in the 1930s. An on-the-ground report from Palm Springs in 1937 wrote, "Western boots are worn to the exclusion of almost everything else."[8] Within a few years, East Coast stores carried them in Western displays. College girls caught on. Square-dancers signed up. Soon, cowboy boots became a well-worn staple of California style.

Opposite: Images of models clad in Western shirts and cowboy boots helped sell everything from steak dinners to cigarettes.

Right: Made for famed cowboy movie star Gene Autry, this boot features leather and lizard skin.

With everyone's eyes on sports culture at Palm Springs, tennis took centre stage. In East Coast clubs, uptight members banned calf-length skirts, then sleeveless shirts, and then butt-skimming tennis dresses. Shorts were one of the most contested garments in fashion history, but women still wore them. "If you gals really knew how cute you look in a well-cut dress, you wouldn't hanker to wear shorts," said one etiquette writer. "You've got to be comfortable, ah, me! Even if you have to insult the aesthetic sense of men to do it? What a pity."[9]

"Function defined fashion in the desert."

On the court, players stuck to white. The Victorian elite chose the colour at the creation of the sport because they believed it was best to disguise sweat stains. Early tennis garb came from private dressmakers or the women players themselves, who purchased commercial patterns through mail-order retailers and made the clothing at home. The tennis wear market blew up in the 1930s with the growth of the sport in California. On the courts at the Racquet Club and Indian Wells, men wore mid-thigh shorts emblazoned with "racing stripes", V-neck tennis sweaters or cable-knit sweaters, which allowed for both warmth and breathability.

As with golfwear, tennis dress was cleverly constructed with gussets and box pleating to allow for mobility. Women wore the styles on and off the court.

Desert

Function defined fashion in the desert. Horseback riding required its own wardrobe and local clubs, such as Desert Riders, used the Cahuilla's trails through the desert. Dude ranches allowed upper-middle-class, mostly white tourists to try on new personas and the associated clothing. Working through tourism publicity firms, the ranch owners advertised in publications ranging from *Vogue* to *Popular Mechanics*. There were five hundred ranches across the country by the early 1940s – sixty-five in California – and 25,000 families visited each year. Palm Springs was home to ranches B-Bar-H, Smoke Tree and Deep Well, among a dozen others.

On these working ranches, "dudes" and "city slickers" dressed in flannel shirts, boots and jeans to clear brush, repair barbed fences and care for farm animals. These stays provided them with first-hand knowledge and a chance to buy. Many came ill-prepared. "After about a week or so, your average dude rancher abandons jodhpurs and silk shirts," a reporter observed in 1924. Instead, the visitor went to town for "cowboys' overalls and tries to resemble the real thing". The Manhattan-based trend forecaster Tobé Report drew a straight line between the ranches and "the popularity of the western cowboy's blue jeans": "Since the crash in '29, Americans discovered dude ranches are an exciting way to spend a summer holiday on less money than the erstwhile popular European tour."[10]

Denim giant Levi Strauss leaned hard into dude ranches as destinations and teaching tools. Every kid in America is taught the story of a miner named Levi Strauss who was forced by necessity to make his own pants during the California Gold Rush of 1848. The tale speaks to Californians' "can do" spirit. In fact, the company invented the story around the Second World War as part of its ever-evolving marketing efforts – a hallmark of its success. In reality, Strauss was a well-known dry goods retailer and distributer.

MURRAY'S DUDE RANCH
VICTORVILLE, CALIF.

The "ONLY NEGRO DUDE RANCH IN THE WORLD."

Murray's was the only California dude ranch for Black people. Operating from 1926 into the 1960s, it was located in Apple Valley, just two hours north-east of Los Angeles, which had quickly become the West Coast city with the largest urban Black population.

Desert

Levi's® original button fly blue jeans-in a den
that shrinks so much, you'll need real faith to buy the
But, oh, what a fit!

**The jeans that won
the West have
discovered women.**

For over a century, the only way a woman could get authentic Levi's 501™ Blue Jeans was to buy a pair made for men. But now, at long last, we've started making those same rugged shrink-to-fit jeans for junior sized women.

Same metal buttons on the fly. Same copper rivets on the front pockets and red

Levi's "tab" on the back pocket. Nothing has been changed but the fit. To fit you perfectly.

**Your washing machine
"tailors" the 501™
to hug every curve.**

What separates 501's™ from the jeans you're accustomed to wearing is our exclusive shrink-to-fit "XXX" all cotton denim. In the store, you'll find that the jeans feel stiff, look dark, and are much bigger than the size indicated.

But trust what we tell yo
just three washings, the b
waist, hips — everything

SHRINKS ABOUT 4" IN WIDTH

SHRINKS ABOUT 4" IN HEIGHT

BEFORE

AFTER

The world. Levi's a registered trademark of Levi Strauss & Co., San Francisco, CA ©1981 Levi Strauss & Co.

Levi's first offered women's clothing in 1918, with their jumpsuit-esque "Freedom-alls." They also offered khaki hiking clothing in 1920s. In 1934, the company the introduced

For the first time since 1850...

WHAT MUST BE THE STRANGEST PAIR OF JEANS EVER MADE ARE FINALLY MADE TO FIT WOMEN.

...ks permanently to fit like ...ans you've ever worn. A ...nore washings, and the ...e "breaks in" to become ...r, lighter in color, and ...ordinarily comfortable.

The older they get ...e better they look.

...a many parts of the world, ...shed-down and broken-in ...of 501™ jeans are more ...rable than a brand new ...Because despite

their after-washing softness, a good old pair of 501's™ is still as tough as nails. (Rumor has it that 501's™ never really die. They just sort of "fade away.")

With their button fly and shrink-to-fit fabric, Levi's 501™ Blue Jeans probably are a little strange.

Look for 501's™ in The Junior Department

But try a pair for yourself. After you've worn the very first blue jeans ever made, you may find everything else running a distant second.

501™

Levi's
WOMENSWEAR

QUALITY NEVER GOES OUT OF STYLE.®

Lady's Levi's jeans, but many women still bought men's 501s. To address the physical differences as outlined in this promotional piece, women's 501s offered more length in the waist and a slimmer leg.

Clint Eastwood sports Westernwear staples such as a saddle-stitched leather belt, shearling vest and a woven falsa blanket in *The Good, The Bad, and The Ugly* (1966).

The company made clothes for loggers cutting down Douglas Fir in Mendocino and for silver miners in Cerro Gordo, where a century-old pair of Levi's was discovered in 2021. By the late 1920s, Americans across the country had seen, heard and read about Levi's denim dungarees.

To distinguish itself in an increasingly crowded jeans market, Levi's advertised extensively and pursued new demographics. With direct competition from Lee (established in 1913) and Wrangler (founded as the Blue Bell Overall Company in 1919), Levi's painted its logo (and an image of two mules trying to pull apart a pair of jeans) on barns and billboards across the country. They sponsored rodeos and radio hours. In the late 1940s, Levi's colourful illustrated magazine advertisements included kids playing with lassos and perky blonde women perched on fences to show off their signature pockets. Levi's pursued women, first offering "Freedom-alls", a jumpsuit-like garment introduced in 1918. In the 1920s, the company made women's hiking clothing out of khaki and sold it all over the West Coast. They launched Lady's Levi's jeans in 1934. True to its founder, Levi's played a tight hand in distribution until the early 1940s. They refused to negotiate price with department store buyers, who deemed the mannish dungarees too stiff for female shoppers and stocked "sports dungarees" in lightweight denim instead.

Working in collaboration with their national retailers in the 1950s, Levi's sponsored fashion shows and hosted onsite "how-to" workshops for assembling a Western wardrobe. They created travelling displays of "Western guns", singer Bing Crosby's denim tuxedo, and bejewelled belt buckles. When finished at one store, the displays went on to the next. At these events, Levi's gave out keychains, magnets and informational pamphlets such as "Going Dude Ranching?". These educational hand-outs offered potential converts advice: "Take a tip from the cowboy on what to wear – and why." The pamphlets detailed how clothing fit into the demands of ranch life. An oilskin pancho is worn over the body and saddle to prevent rain from getting into the seat. When not in use, the pancho protects blankets and gear. As for the prerequisite cuffed jean bottoms, they are "sometimes used as an extra pocket for matches, nails, etc.".

Desert

501s

Levi's 501 jeans are the most famous pants in the world. Durability is key to their success. The use of copper rivets to reinforce areas where the garment wore thin was the idea of Strauss's business partner Jacob Davis, a tailor based in Reno, Nevada. The two took out a patent on the process in 1873, and marked the jeans with "501" to distinguish them as their highest-grade product. The "flat-felled" seams are made by folding two raw edges over onto themselves before stitching them together. Zippers were introduced into menswear in the mid-1930s, but Levi's didn't make a zippered version of the 501 until 1954, when it started to develop its East Coast market.

Levi's likes to celebrate the history of 501s through its advertising, including a 1998 campaign featuring the famous shot of Marlon Brando wearing 501s and a white T-shirt in *The Wild One* (1953). The copy reads: "Our models can beat up their models."

Hollywood movies brought California's subcultures to the world. Marlon Brando's *The Wild One* popularized white T-shirts and 501 jeans.

chapter 4

HiGHWAY

California style was test driven on the Golden State's 400,000 miles of roads. From Highway 1 that snakes along the coast to the famed Rodeo Drive, a vast system of highways, freeways, expressways, streets and roads made Californians mobile. This ever-evolving and highly regulated infrastructure allowed beachgoers, golfers and weekend adventurers to have an alpine picnic, take to the links or hike in the desert, and has appeared in countless movies as more than just a way of getting from A to B, but as an essential romantic and momentous character in the California landscape.

"An essential romantic and momentous character in the California landscape."

Casual clothing, a national phenomenon with strong roots in California, accommodated life in a car. The state's burgeoning fashion industry put out well-proportioned pants, rubber-soled shoes and cardigans for when it cooled off at night. Cars and highways also came to define shopping in California, from downtown department stores, to beachside boutiques, to the iconic shopping mall.

Highway

California culture centred around the automobile. The omnipresent sunglasses were a central accessory to life on the road, as seen on Patricia Arquette in *True Romance* (1993).

California's car culture required easy-to-wear sportswear, such as this silk jersey shirt by Italian Emilio Pucci, seen here with a model in a 1964 Buick Electra. I. Magnin sold exclusive European sportswear to a discerning California crowd.

This 1983 image of the Monte Cristo Car Club speaks to the role of the automobile in Latino culture in Southern California. It was part of a Pulitzer Prize-winning series of essays, art, and images called "Latinos" by the *Los Angeles Times*.

California "has grown up with the automobile," according to an executive of The Automobile Club, an advocacy group for transportation and tourism founded in 1900.[1] Cars were essential to the California dream of single-family homes with backyards that were just a short drive to a shopping centre. This veneration of what we now call "lifestyle" is written into the heart of the state's allure. In 1903, Charles Lummis, a journalist and lover of California who wrote more than four hundred books and articles on the region, pinpointed the differences between coasts: "Eastern cities are swelling with Americans who move in to make Money." Yet, the country and cities of California are "filling with Americans who move in to make a Life". To Lummis, "In a word, this is the Chosen Country."[2]

Highway

California's driving culture defined both rural and urban development. In car-crazy Los Angeles, the placement of highways directly determined what tracts of land were developed, who got public transportation, and where people of colour could live. The most powerful players in the city orchestrated this complicated process, and systematically segregated Mexican, Asian, and Black residents from the affluent white ones through restrictive clauses. Highways united and divided.

In car ownership, Los Angelenos were immediately ahead of the game. By 1910, the city had the highest per capita rate in the world, owning one car for every eight residents. The national mean was one per forty-three citizens. The city's thriving tyre business, home to major manufacturers Goodyear and Firestone, was routinely blamed for the lack of garment workers. A secondary economy catered to car maintenance needs. City directories show 170 gas stations in 1920, almost 700 in 1925, and more than 1,500 in 1930. Nearly a century later, there are thirty-one million cars registered in the state.[3]

During internment, Japanese Americans were forced to work on farms to assure economic stability for the United States during its war efforts, as this government-produced image documents. The workers wore overalls, sunglasses and slouchy hats to pick oranges, lettuce and almonds that were taken by trucks to train depots. Roads were primary to economic success.

One of California's most famous state parks, Big Basin Redwoods Park provided the setting for pivotal scenes in *Vertigo* (1958). Filmed just 15 miles down the road from Alfred Hitchcock's second home in the California mountains, the film features costumes designed by industry grande dame, Edith Head.

Whether driving to the country club or an alpine resort, Californians used their highways and leisure time to connect with nature. Roads linked them to a sprawling network of city, state and national parks. Hiking called for gabardine pants with patch pockets and crushable hats with names such as "The Californian" and "The Santa Cruz", which had snaps for convertible brims. City parks flourished. San Diego purchased land in the 1920s and turned it into an enviable system of city parks. The three-hundred-acre McLaren Park in San Francisco was built during the Depression by the Works Progress Administration (WPA), a government funded programme that used unemployed men to complete public works. The park boasted a pool, hiking trails and a golf course. Founded in 1902, Big Basin Redwoods Park was the first state park, followed by hundreds more including Old Town in San Diego and Folsom Lake. Today, more than two hundred Californian parks welcome seventy million visitors a year.

Overleaf: Complete with extra padding at the waist and elbows and a collar that can be snapped into various positions, the motorcycle jacket was born of practicality in the late 1910s. It came into California subculture alongside the bike itself in the late 1940s, and became internationally famous with films such as *Rebel Without a Cause* (1955) and *Grease* (1978).

Highway

Shorts

Shorts had a specific purpose: to allow for freedom of movement. They were spurred to popularity by the bicycling craze of the 1930s, and worn by women to garden, to shop, to pick up the kids and to do housework. California manufacturers made every variety. In 1938, the *Boston Post* commented on the infiltration of this California-born trend: "Husbands no longer come home and deliver stern lectures upon finding their wives cooking supper in shorts. It's just taken for granted."[4]

Shorts are central to California style. By the early 1950s, the fashion industry named the varying lengths according to the islands that supposedly inspired them, with "Jamaica" as the shortest, the mid-thigh "Nassau" cut, and "Bermudas" that came to above the knee. Bermudas made it to stateside vacation spots in the late 1930s and then spread like wildfire across college campuses for both men and women. Men's use of shorts met with little regulation, but women in shorts prompted stern words from the dean and written clarifications of the dress code. With a wardrobe built on sportswear, Californians paid little attention to shorts on California's golf courses and tennis courts.

California style was made for life on the roads – relaxed-fit pants, sweaters, tennis shoes and culottes. By the 1930s, the garments made and popularized in California were swept up in a national movement towards what a journalist called "the casual effect everyone is trying to achieve". Born of a growing middle class and an increasingly efficient fashion industry, sartorial standards allowed sport coats to replace suit jackets. Girdles stayed in the back of the drawer. Never having given much credence to East Coast fashion dictates, Californians remained at the vanguard of casual dress.

Teenagers sunbathe on the hood of their stalled
car on the Santa Monica highway in 1980.

Long hair and loud music defined the music scene of Los Angeles in the first half of the 1980s. Participants and observers paired vintage T-shirts and stone-washed jeans, a California-invented process that involves caustic chemicals and at least a dozen washings.

Golfwear

Golf has played a central role in the development of California style and American sportswear. It first spawned menswear trends such as the Norfolk suit and spectator shoes, the predecessor of saddle shoes. Printed socks, V-neck sweaters and tweed knickers also came from the course. By the mid-1910s, retailers sold clothing specifically for golf.

East Coast country clubs were not a place for avant-garde fashion to flourish. For decades, many forbade shorts in the dining room and bikinis at the pool. California's interpretations of golfwear were, unsurprisingly, less uptight. Where East Coasters went for tweeds and wool, West Coasters dressed in cotton, jersey knits or white linen. Named for one of Scotland's sweater-friendly Shetland Islands, the Fair Isle, with its decorative crew neckline, was a common sight on California courses. So were the loose-gauge cardigans made in knitting mills just up the coast. At Monterey's Del Monte Golf Course (founded in 1897), club members usually wore pants, but in typical Californian style they liked brightly coloured madras, a lightweight cotton fabric in mismatching plaids. Patterned golfwear was big in California.

Catalina Island had been inhabited for 7,000 years by sea-faring tribes including the Gabrielino/Tongva. In the late 1880s, colonists began a tourism industry that commandeered the island. To attract sports enthusiasts, business owners produced brochures such as this one.

California's highways also helped shoppers to shop. The options seemed limitless: surf shops carrying synthetic rubber, neoprene wetsuits; the atelier of local master Michael Novarese offering hand-beaded eveningwear; vintage vendors selling their treasures at Rose Bowl Flea Market. A never-ending stream of tourists purchased clothing all over the state – the stalls on Los Angeles's Olvera Street; the beachy boutiques of Monterey; the revolutionary, fashion-focused Echelon Mall in San Diego; and San Francisco's Maiden Lane, a red-light district that was turned into a pedestrian shopping district to avoid noisy cars and buses.

All over California, towns and cities used urban development to facilitate car-friendly retail shopping. When Wilshire Boulevard's "Miracle Mile" shopping district was conceived in the mid-1920s, it seemed a laughable distance away from downtown. Anchored by the May Company's famed chrome-faced Streamline Moderne building (1939), the district's signage was designed to be read through a windshield. A hotspot for menswear with retailers Desmond's and Silverwoods, Miracle Mile was also home to The Broadway, Ohrbach's, Phelps-Terkel and Myer Siegel & Co. Everyone provided parking, a must-have for modern shopping.

Bullocks Wilshire was front and centre in Miracle Mile, a 230,000 square-foot Art Deco emporium designed by father-son duo, the Parkinsons. It was a joint venture between John Bullock and fellow Canadian immigrant P.G. Winnett, and became a powerhouse in California retailing. The store's main entrance faced the parking lot, not the street. Winnett attended the 1925 Art Deco exhibition in Paris and saw the work of Sonia Delaunay, a famed textile designer. He hired her to do the carpets and upholstery for the shoe salon. The *Beverly Hills Citizen* proclaimed that between their Golden Triangle (Wilshire Boulevard, Canon Drive and Santa Monica Boulevard) and nearby Miracle Mile, "Fifth Avenue has come to Los Angeles."[5]

This knit tunic by California-born Bonnie Cashin
features a hood for driving in a convertible.

Business casual

Khaki fit the needs of California's car culture. This durable, brown cotton twill was first used by British soldiers in mid-nineteenth century India. In the Second World War, the "Class C" army uniform used cloth produced by North Carolina-based Galey & Lord, makers of Cramerton Army Cloth. Worn by men serving in the Pacific Rim, khaki was light and quick-drying. Upon return, the men did not want to give up their khakis. The fabric withstood wrinkles, stains and washing. Cut with an ample seat, khakis were great for driving. California menswear makers flooded the market with well-made options.

In the early 1980s, Californians' predilection for khakis interfaced again with cultural change. Tech firms of Silicon Valley began to prioritize "performance" over "propriety". As a result, office dress codes that had been held in place by human-resources managers and a lingering old guard slowly died. What replaced these outdated rules was "business casual", a middle ground with a lot more personal freedom. This distinctly American genre of dress spread across the world with "dress-down Fridays" in the 1990s, and became standard office attire in the 2000s.

Levi Strauss launched its Dockers brand in the mid-1980s. The company's well-oiled publicity machine pushed the brand to the forefront of "business casual" with informational pamphlets sent to human resources managers and advertisements in Times Square.

DOCKERS

Autumn
1992

For the store nearest you call
1-800-DOCKERS

I. Magnin was a West Coast-born department store that
thrived on unique merchandise and catered specifically to
Californians. Their flagship on Union Square became San
Francisco's shopping mecca with an "imposing exterior
beauty" and "breath-taking interior magnificence". An
architecture journalist reported that on each of the ten floors
there "are skillful groupings of exquisite correlated shops,
which flow logically into each other and make shopping
easy, intimate, and pleasant". The store featured two dozen
varieties of marble and special lights for looking at the colour
of furs.[6] The savvy Magnin family set up branch stores to
catch the tourist trade at Hotel del Coronado (1914), the
Biltmore Hotel (1927) and others. Their world-class location
on Wilshire Boulevard was conceived around a two-hundred-
car parking lot, making it, as one store executive bragged,
"so completely Californian in concept".[7] The building was
designed by local architects Myron Hunt and H.C. Chambers
and opened in 1938, with a front of white Yule marble
quarried in Colorado and a polished black granite base. It
was the first store in the country to be fully air-conditioned.
I. Magnin had fifteen thriving branches in 1966.

I. Magnin's Wilshire location was home to arguably the best custom
boutique run by Stella Hanania. Trained under Bernard Newman of
the custom shop at Manhattan's Bergdorf Goodman, the Beirut-born
couturier created women's suits, dresses and gowns for Hollywood
stars and society women. This dress suit belonged to Corinne
Entratter Sidney, widow of famed musical director George Sidney.

Beverly Hills was a shopping destination that beckoned movie stars, millionaires and sightseers from Syracuse, but gave them few places to park. A city within the larger metropolis of Los Angeles, Beverly Hills had a city council and Chamber of Commerce hell-bent on getting more people into the shopping district. They tried parking validation and a successful trolly system to shuttle in the tourists.

Tourism was the lifeblood of Beverly Hills. Some bought; others just gawked. "Hospitality is part of the Rodeo Drive way," reminded Fred Hayman, the legendary owner of Giorgio Beverly Hills, known for its yellow-and-white striped awnings and namesake perfume. By the late 1980s, tourists were about half of the city's retail business. "The day you don't welcome tourists," he said, "is the day you go down the tubes."[8]

Few bastions of consumerism glisten as brightly as the California shopping mall. After the Second World War, the popularity of downtown stores dimmed. In 1924, nearly half of all people going into the Los Angeles central business district arrived by automobile, and more than 75 per cent of department store purchases were made downtown. By 1939, it had dropped to 54 per cent of those purchases and by 1956, only 23 per cent of department store purchases were made downtown. As city planners, Chambers of Commerce members and economists will attest, Californians wanted their shopping to be convenient. Retail executives learned quickly that highways could take shoppers both toward and away from the city.

Budget-friendly Sears anchored many shopping centres in
California. By the mid-1970s, Sears had nearly nine hundred
stores nationally and nearly half a million employees.

"California is a new country, a modern country, a country open to contemporary ideas," declared architect Victor Gruen, the father of the shopping mall. Having fled Austria after its annexation by the Nazis in 1938, Gruen ended up in the States, and made his new home in California. Gruen believed that California "means informal living with an accent on outdoor activities"[9]. In the 1920s, roadside pull-ins offered groceries and gasoline, alongside locksmiths or cobblers. By the 1940s, out-of-town shopping centres, complete with parking lots and plenty of signage, became home to branch locations of downtown retailers, shoe stores and hair salons.

Gruen's work in West Coast department store chains such as Grayson-Robinson pioneered open-concept retailing. Rather than waiting for a salesperson, customers freely touched merchandise and made their way to manned checkout points. Gruen's stores made access to goods and freedom of personal choice the hallmarks of modern consumerism. The 1956 creation of Minnesota's Southdale Center, the world's first enclosed mall, brought radical change in how and where Americans shopped. Gruen's firm oversaw the construction of more than fifty malls around the country, including a dozen in California. The malls of Southern California garnered national attention for the Valley Girl subculture in the early 1980s. Deriving much of their style from the region's vibrant dance culture, Valley Girls wore jean mini-skirts, colour-blocked sweatshirts, paint-splattered leggings, high-ponytails and their signature leg warmers, the look coming to embody an era of colourful, optimistic consumerism.

The California shopping mall is both a commercial and a cultural centre. In movies such as 1983's *Valley Girl*, teen girls sport two-tone jackets, athletic wear including headbands, sweatbands and leg warmers, and bold, graphic makeup.

Highway

Pedal pushers

Pedal pushers are tapered, calf-length pants that revolutionized womenswear. An early maker of culottes, DeDe Johnson was a sportswear designer who moonlighted in Hollywood, making patio dresses for June Cleaver on the television show *Leave it to Beaver*. With the help of celebrity followers Audrey Hepburn and Marilyn Monroe, Johnson pushed her bicycle-friendly pants into women's wardrobes. In 1944, she received a plaque for her invention from the California Fashion Creators, a collaborative group of fashion designers.

California staked a claim to popularizing pants for women. In the late 1920s, California makers produced frontier pants, bib-front numbers with large buttons, followed by sailor-inspired bell-bottoms. By the mid-1930s, denim dungarees became popular for gardening and outdoor adventures. In the 1940s, "slacks" of wool and rayon gabardine mimicked the look of men's trousers. Johnson's pedal pushers joined Capri pants and clam diggers as dressier options for suburban moms.

Longtime fashion editor of the *Los Angeles Times*, Sylva Weaver insisted, "California alone was responsible for putting women in pants."[10] While lumped together in the category of short pants, Capris, clam diggers and pedal pushers each had their own length and degree of tapering.

chapter 5

EPILOGUE

Rapper Tupac Shakur enthusiastically wore the creations of Karl Kani, the brand of New York-raised designer Carl Williams. Williams began selling oversized jeans through advertisements in the back of hip-hop magazines. He moved to California with what he called "$1,000 and a dream", where he became a favourite of rappers, celebrities and athletes.

"California is not just a State; California is a way of life"

Architect Victor Gruen in 1945[1]

The world wants a piece of California. We want its technology from the start-ups of Silicon Valley and the medical labs of its world-class universities. Its innovations have given us tighter sweaters and faster smartphones. We want its entertainment. We want Mötley Crüe with their leather pants along with San Francisco's the Grateful Dead in tie-dye T-shirts and bare feet. We want Tupac Shakur, his 'California Love' and his bandana, tied in the front. We want California's omnipresent television. *Baywatch* had more than a billion viewers at its pinnacle in the mid-1990s. We want its *Falcon Crest* shoulder pads and the plumped up lips of *The Real Housewives of Orange County*, and to keep up with the Kardashians. We want Mickey Mouse.

California style is born of place. This book celebrates the material and creative advantages that make California fashion thrive. These clothes are built for doing stuff, for picking strawberries or dancing along with your workout tape. Even transplants grow in California's glow: British brand Reebok cashed in on the region's aerobics craze with the padded, high-top "Freestyle", the first athletic shoe for women. Thanks to American distribution and regional production, Reebok went from $13 million in sales in 1982 to $307 million in 1985. Old traditions endured alongside new ones: sportswear maker Esprit de Corps made the brightly coloured sweaters for which San Francisco is known, and paired them with cotton-spandex leggings. Founded by Susie Tompkins Buell and her husband Doug (who went on to start The North Face), Esprit was at the vanguard of corporate culture in the 1980s, with a pet-friendly office, restaurant, gym, and small park that is now owned by the city.

Epilogue

Above: Making the most of the sand and the cement,
this enthusiast skateboards to a surfing spot. His nearly
demolished tennis shoes complement the shorts, strategically
ripped at the inner seam to allow for mobility.

Opposite: Kylie and Kendall Jenner lean hard into traditional
elements of California style: the chunky silver concho belt,
turquoise jewellery, cut-off jeans, work boots and bootie shorts.
The sisters are seen here at the 2015 Coachella music festival
held in a historic railroad town south of Palm Springs.

Above: The neighbourhood around the intersection of Haight and Ashbury Streets in San Francisco welcomed progressive thinkers and dressers.

Opposite: Co-opting traditional ideas of masculine, working-class dress, the "Castro clone" subculture established many of the queer-signalling staples celebrated today.

Born in San Francisco's Castro district, the 1970s post-Stonewall "clone" look can still be seen on the gay scene today. An emulation of hypermasculine semaphores such as well-fit Levi's, moustaches, white T-shirts and plaid flannel shirts, the look subverted traditional masculinity and many of the emblematic pieces of California men's style, and provided an escape from the stereotypes imposed on the queer community by straight society at large.[2]

Epilogue

Style also came in the form of the uniform of political dissent. Founded in Oakland, the Black Panther Party were instantly recognizable with their members in black leather, berets and hair worn in natural Afros. Far from being a fashion statement, these choices were made to confront the racist powers that be, and challenge the idea of the "acceptable" way to campaign for civil rights. The look was later referenced by Beyoncé and her dancers in her epic 2016 Super Bowl half-time show, in a radical tribute to Black power.

The beach remains central to the creation of California style. Beachwear is big business. International conglomerate Kayser-Roth bought both Catalina and Cole of California. Rose Marie Reid sold her company to New Jersey-based Jonathan Logan, who made a dozen lines at 39 production centres and sold to 5,000 retailers. Beachwear brands struggle to find the balance between authenticity and commercial success. Today, California's surf brands have international fame: Ocean Pacific; Body Glove; La Blanca; Hang Ten; O'Neill and Hurley.

Activist Kathleen Cleaver served as Communications Secretary of the Black Panther Party, a political organization born in 1966 to engender the self-determination of Black communities. Male and female Panthers wore natural hairstyles, turtlenecks, leather jackets and sunglasses. The Panthers were born in Oakland, a city that nurtured and popularized many of the urban styles associated with California.

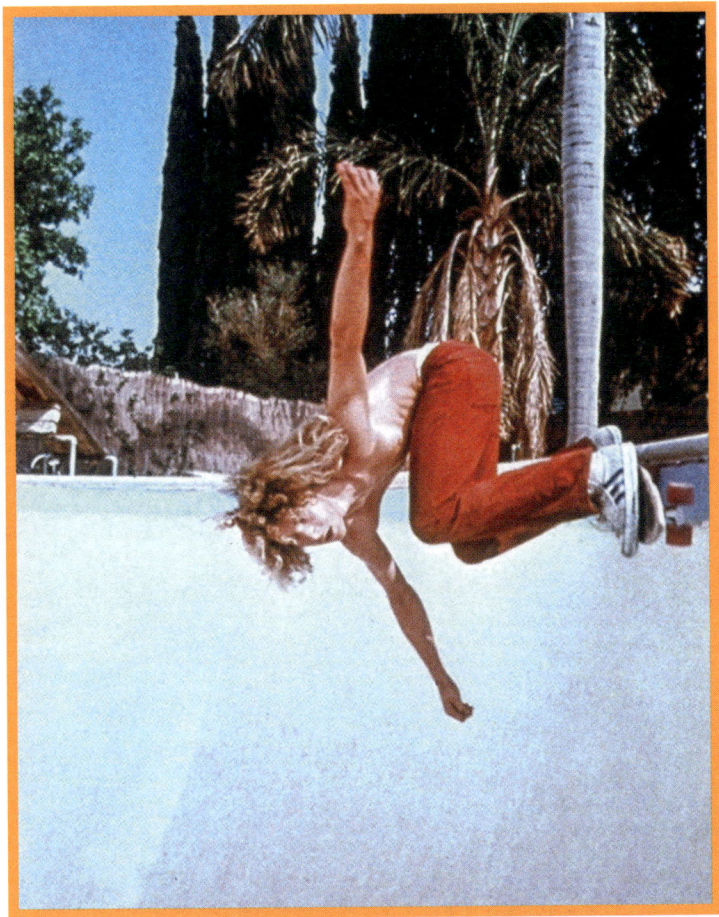

Above: Tony Alva skating a drained swimming pool in the
2001 documentary *Dogtown and Z-Boys*, about the pioneering
of 1970s Zephyr skating, directed by Stacy Peralta.

Opposite: California's TYR gained global followers when they custom-made
suits for the cast of *Baywatch*, which ran from 1989 to 2001. Seen here,
the beach's unofficial spokesmodel, Canadian-born Pamela Anderson.

Now the fourth largest economy in the world, California has more than 30 million registered cars and 39 million residents. Highways take shoppers to the mall and families to the beach. They are also tools for division, cutting up neighbourhoods to ensure racial, ethnic and socio-economic segregation. California's built environment inspires human creativity. Half-transportation, half-sport, skateboarding came from the streets and grew up in the drained swimming pools of vacant houses during a real estate crisis. Vans' tagline "Off the Wall" reminds us of that history. California's thriving lowrider scene venerates the automobile, well-coiffed hair and cuffed jeans in dark denim. Created by Mexican Americans in post-war Los Angeles, lowriding was "more than merely a 'car-oriented' subculture". An anthropologist explained in 1975 that the car itself was "the fundamental basis of social organization and the primary vehicle of self-expression".[3] Fashion came a close second.

The nearly 270 million people who visit California each year no longer need wardrobe advice from salespeople at I. Magnin. The store was absorbed by Macy's in the mid 1990s, anyway. Today, a global fashion industry serves up California style. Patagonia, founded by rock climbers in Ventura, revolutionized outerwear. It produces its famed Nano Puff model fleece vest in Sri Lanka and sells it to tech bros around the world. Another mountain-born brand, The North Face was the first to embrace waterproof Gore-Tex to improve climbing, camping and ski gear. Their "Made in America" collection sells alongside the clothing produced in Vietnam. Snowboarding is now used to sell soda, skull caps and quilted parkas, but its origins in California's outdoor life endear it to tens of millions who have never – and will never – try the sport. Snowboarding's fashion influence has been seen on the runways of Milan and the streets of Tokyo.

Oversized hoop earrings, blinged-out nails and dark lip liner defines Chola style – a creation of second generation Mexican-American women that has spread from East Los Angeles around the world.

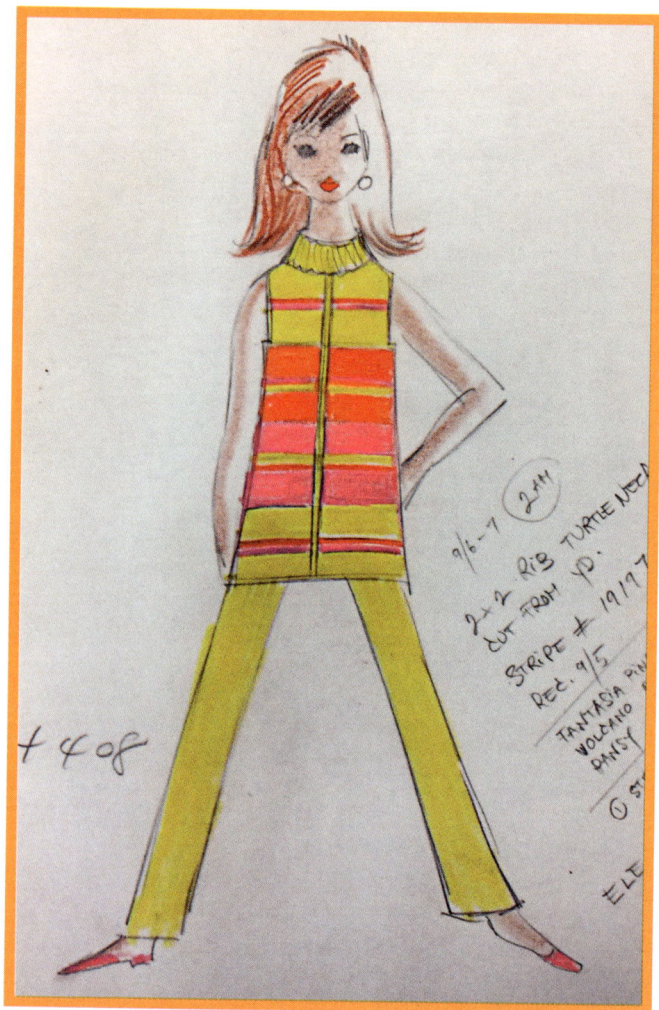

Berlin-born Irene Saltern designed this tunic ensemble for Phil Rose. Saltern and her husband were refugees from Nazi Germany to Los Angeles, where she worked as a costume designer before moving into a successful tenure with Tabak of California.

From its days on the dude ranches of Palm Springs, Western wear has remained central to California style. It feeds on personalization: well-worn cowboy boots and a leather belt with carved silver accents paired with leggings or a long white skirt or jeans. Levi's remains a cultural powerhouse, but California has been home to high-end denim brands since the days of Marjorie Montgomery's faded denim frontier pants. The industrial town of Vernon, just outside of Los Angeles, produces denim and sews garments for dozens of jean makers. Over the decades, their products went around the world as Jordache, Guess? Jeans, Lucky Brand and 7 For All Mankind. Bronx-born Ralph Lauren built an empire on his interpretation of California style, complete with strategically faded jean jackets, embellished with Mexican-inspired, floral embroidery. When useful, he borrowed from Indigenous cultures, whose artists continuously push back on fashion companies using their names and traditions with varying degrees of success.

Much like the state itself, California style exalts individualism. Its mishmash of beloved garments and accessories has visual resonance around the world: the string bikini; flip-flops; polo shirts; yoga pants; tube tops; cargo shorts; Uggs; jeans with the butt decorated in faux gems. If Paris has given fashion with a capital "F" the gold standard for craftsmanship and New York created clothing that is a working vocabulary for city chic, what has California contributed? Freedom.

FOOTNOTES

Introduction

1 "Editor's Note", *California Stylist*, February 1939, 5.

2 "Los Angeles Little Cutters", *Fortune*, May 1945, 182.

3 "Personality Sketch – Joseph Zukin", *California Stylist*, February 1939, 2.

4 Henry W. Louis, "Los Angeles Garments Set Styles", *Southern California Business*, September 1922, 115.

5 For statistics on tourism, see Todd Gish, "Growing and Selling Los Angeles: The All-Year Club of Southern California, 1921–1941", *Southern California Quarterly*, Winter 2007–2008, 391–415.

6 Rose Pesotta, *Bread Upon the Waters*, New York: Mead & Co, 1944, 48.

7 "Stars in Your Window", *California Stylist*, August 1945.

8 Norris Willatt, "New Look in Women's Wear", *Barron's*, June 4, 1962, 23.

9 "Country Has Come to Recognize", *Women's Wear Daily*, May 21, 1937, section 3, 2.

Chapter 1: The Beach

1 Marjorie Cherry to parents, 30 April 1930, Marjorie Cherry Rohfleisch Papers, Schlesinger Library, Harvard University, Cambridge, Mass.

2 "California Knitwear Manufacturers Emerge as Increasingly Important", *Knitted Outwear Times*, May 6, 1937.

3 Frances Piaget, "Fashions", *The Berkeley Gazette*, August 2, 1929, 14.

4 "Enter Evening Pajamas", *New York Times*, June 16, 1935, X6.

5 "Sportswear Sales Volume Heavy", *Women's Wear Daily*, January 28, 1943, 16.

6 David Barry, "Every Day is Sun Day", *Women's Wear Daily*, September 1, 1976, 20.

7 "Lastex Brings Fit and Fashion to Swimwear", *California Stylist*, February 1955, 38.

8 For more on Rose Marie Reid, see the thesis of Molly Hartvigsen, "Rose Marie Reid: Swimsuit Visionary", Fashion Institute of Technology, State University of New York, 2021.

9 *Idaho Daily Statesman*, April 8, 1950, 23.

10 R. L. Rutsky, "Surfing the Other", *Film Quarterly*, Summer, 1999, 14.

11 Mark McFee, *Fast and Furious: The Story of American International Pictures*, Jefferson, N. C.: MacFarland, 1984, 144.

12 Duke Boyd, "The Duke of Surf Wear", *Waikiki* magazine, January 3, 2014; "Hang Ten Dives in Swimwear", *Women's Wear Daily*, July 1, 1998.

13 Oral history with Maurice Levin conducted by Gail Stein on February 18, 2000 at the Los Angeles County Museum of Art Special Collections; Sylvia Sheppard, "Young California", *Women's Wear Daily*, June 16, 1965, 5.

Chapter 2: Mountains

1 Reverand E. Graham, "Letters from Southern California", *New York Observer and Chronicle*, November 25, 1875, 376.

2 G. Vallejo, "Ranch and Mission Days", *The Century Magazine*, December 1890.

3 H. Wisby, "Camping Out with an Automobile", *Outing*, March, 1905, 739.

4 P. J. Schwab, "Camping is an Art!", *Sunset* May 1927, 20.

5 Agnes Edward Partin, letter to parents, 2 March 1918, Agnes Edward Partin Papers, University Archives, University of California at Berkeley, Berkeley, CA.

6 "See Peak Skiwear", *Women's Wear Daily*, September 1939, 19.

7 "Peacetime Dividends From Wartime Research", Radio

Business Forum presented by Commerce and Industry Association of New York, February 9, 1946, Station WMCA 1657.

Chapter 3: Desert

1   M. Kast, "Dude Ranching in the United States", *The Southwestern Social Science Quarterly*, June 1941, 33.

2   A pamphlet from Levi's called "Gone Dude Ranching" is part of an unprocessed collection at the Special Collections of FDIM in Los Angeles.

3   Sylva Weaver, "California Hues to Dot the Countryside", *Los Angeles Times*, October 17, 1937, D 15.

4   Cindy S. Aron, *Working at Play: The History of Vacations in the United States*, New York: Oxford University Press, 1999, 238.

5   Sylva Weaver, "California Hues to Dot the Countryside", *Los Angeles Times*, October 17, 1937, D 15.

6   "Plunging Necklines in Male Styles", *Los Angeles Times*, October 28, 1957.

7   "Stylized for the Californian", *San Francisco Chronicle*, February 1, 1941, 22.

8   "Palm Springs in Ranch Clothes!", *Women's Wear Daily*, February 24, 1937, 6.

9   K.U. Witan, *Lady Lore*, Lawrence, KS: The World Press, 1939, 17.

10 "Desert Gains as Mecca of Vast Tourism", *Women's Wear Daily*, November 27, 1924, 4; Tobé Report, August 8, 1942, 3.

Chapter 4: Highway

1   Ed Ainsworth, "Out of the Noose!", (Los Angeles: Automobile Club of Southern California, 1939), 1.

2   Lummis, "Right Hand of the Continent", *Out West*, August 1902, 154.

3   Scott L. Bottles, *Los Angeles and the Automobile: The Making of the Modern City*. Berkeley, CA: University of California

Press, 1987, 57; Richard W. Longstreth, "Drive-In, the Supermarket, and the Transformation of Commercial Space in Los Angeles, 1914–1941", Boston: MIT Press, 1999, 128.

4   "College Shoes", *Boot and Shoe Recorder*, July 6, 1935.

5   "May Company Wilshire Yields District into Shopping Unit", *Beverly Hills Citizen*, September 8, 1939.

6   "Beauty, Comfort and Convenience", *P.G. and E. Progress*, February 1948, 3.

7   T. Ross Anderson, Speech to Federated Board of Directors, October 16, 1975. SFH 2, Series V: Stores, I. Magnin Collection, San Francisco Public Library.

8   G. Abrams, "A Street Named Desire", *The Los Angeles Times*, November 20, 1990, E1-E11.

9   Victor Gruen, "The California Look in Store Design", *California Men's Stylist*, April 1945, 81.

10 Sylva Weaver, "Queen of the Style Seas Nears Southland Port", *Los Angeles Times*, September 17, 1941.

Chapter 5: Epilogue

1   Victor Gruen, "The California Look in Store Design", *California Men's Stylist*, April 1945, 81.

2   https://www.gq.com/story/70s-clone-look-queer-clothing

3   J. Allard Holtz, "The Low-Riders: Portrait of an Urban Youth Subculture," *Youth and Society*; June 1975; 6.

iNDEX

Page numbers in italic refer to captions

Aarons, Slim *91*
Adrian 28, 29, *51*
Alva, Tony *149*
Anderson, Pamela *149*
après-ski 77, 78, *79*
Aron, Cindy *93*
Arquette, Patricia *110*
Asher, William 52
Autry, Gene *97*

Back to the Future 26, *27*
Baldwin Hills *16*
bandanas 87
Barron's 25
Baywatch 141, *149*
Beach Boys, the 53, *56*
Beach Party 52
Bell, Rex *93*
Beverly Hills 29, 132
Beverly Hills Cop 31
Beyoncé *147*
bikinis 53, 124, 153
Bill & Ted's Excellent Adventure 31
Black Panther Party 147, *147*
boots 31, 63, 64, 68, 97, *97*, 153
Bow, Clara 29, *93*
Boyd, Duke 58
Brando, Marlon 106, *106*
Bullock's 48, 89, 126
Burton *81*

Cahuilla people 84, 87, 100
cars 68, 110–119
Casa California 89
Cashin, Bonnie 13, *64*, 127
Castro district 144, *144*
Catalina 38, 45, *44*, 48, *49*, 58, *124*

Cher 32
Cherry, Marjorie 38
Chola style 09, *151*
Chouinard, Yvon 68
Clancy 38
Cleaver, June 136
Cleaver, Kathleen *147*
Clueless 31, *33*
Coachella Valley 84, *142*
Coffman, Nellie 89
Cohn-Goldwater 67
Cole of California 25, 45, 48, *49*
Crawford, Joan 28, 48
Crosby, Bing 105
Cross Colours 31, *31*

Davis, Jacob 106
denim 13, 26, *27*, 64, 104, 105, 153
Desert Inn and Sanitorium 89, *94*
DeWeese, Mary Ann 45
Dietrich, Marlene 29
Dimmitt, Viola 13, 89
Dockers *128*
Dogtown and Z-Boys 149
dude ranches 100, *101*, 105
DuPont 38

Eastwood, Clint *104*
Eggers, Henry L. *12*
Entratter Sidney, Corinne *131*
eveningwear 43
Everson, Cory 32

Falcon Crest 141
Fast Times at Ridgemont High 31
Fellegi, Margit 48
Fern Shoe Company 46
flannel 64, 67

Fortune magazine 10
Freedom-alls *102*, 105
Fresh Prince of Bel Air, The 31, *31*

Galanos, James 24, 29
Galey & Lord 128
Galitzine, Irene 77
Gantner California 71
Garland, Judy 28
Gaynor, Janet 29
Gibsonville 63
Gidget 53
golf 10, 99,117, 120, 124
Good, The Bad and The Ugly, The 104
Gore-Tex *150*
GQ 09
Grae, Viola *93*
Grand Hotel 28
Grease 117
Greer, Howard 29
Gruen, Victor 135, 141
Guess Jeans 26, *27*, 153

Hanania, Stella *131*
Hang Ten 58, *147*
Harlow, Jean 48
hats 14, 87, *114*
Hawk, Tony 80
Hayman, Fred 132
Head, Edith *78*, *116*
Hepburn, Audrey 136
Hitchcock, Alfred *116*
Hollywood 26, 29, 48
How to Stuff a Wild Bikini 53

InStyle 26

Jackets 26, *27*, 68, 117
jeans 100, 105, *122*, *142*, 153
Jenner, Kendall *142*

Jenner, Kylie *142*
John, Elton *32*
Johnson, DeDe *136*
Joyce *46, 46*
jumpsuits *67, 77*

Kani, Karl *140*
khaki *14, 102, 105, 128*
Klein, Calvin *33*
Knitted Outerwear Times 40
knitwear *71, 72*
Korfanta, Karen *74*
Kurvz Extremewear *81*

L'Tanya *42*
Lady's Levi's *102, 105*
Lastex *48, 51*
Lauren, Ralph *153*
Levi Strauss *14, 25, 87, 100,
  102, 103, 104, 105, 106,
  106, 128, 128, 144*
loafers *87*
Los Angeles *14, 16, 22, 22, 31,
  45, 67, 114, 132, 150, 151*
Los Angeles Times 90, *113, 137*

Mabs of Hollywood *48, 49*
Macy's *150*
Magnin, I. *21, 77, 131, 131, 150*
Mammoth Mountain *74*
masks *87*
Masters, Addie *12, 13*
Max, Barney *89*
May, Mona *33*
Men's Apparel Guild in
  California *90, 94*
menswear *71, 90, 94, 95, 106,
  124, 126, 128*
Mexico *17, 18, 19, 19, 21, 22,
  48, 84*
Mickey Mouse *141*
Midler, Bette *32*
Miracle Mile *126*
Monroe, Marilyn *136*
Monte Cristo Car Club *113*
Montgomery, Marjorie
  13, 153
Murray's dude ranch *101*

Muscle Beach Party 53
music scene *122*
Myers, Elizabeth *13*

Neutra, Richard *91*
New York Times 43
Newman, Bernard *131*
North Face, The *68, 141, 150*
Novarese, Michael *29, 126*
Nowitzky, Mary *43*
nylon *77, 77*

Oakland *147, 147*
Ohrbach's *126*
Orry-Kelly *29*
Outing 68

pajamas *14, 43, 43*
Palm Springs *87, 89–90, 91,
  99, 100, 142, 153*
Patagonia *68, 68, 150*
Patou, Jean *77*
pedal pushers *136–7*
Pendleton *56*
Peralta, Stacy *149*
Photoplay 26
pitons *68*
ponchos *104, 105*
Poolside Gossip 91
Pretty Woman 31
Pucci, Emilio *77, 112*

Reagan, Nancy *24*
*Real Housewives of Orange
  County, The* 141
Rebel Without a Cause 117
Reebok *141*
Reid, Rose Marie *53, 147*
Rodeo Ben *93*
Rodeo Drive *110, 132*
Rose, Phil *152*
Rossignolm *81*
Round Up fashion event *90,
  94, 95*

Saltern, Irene *152*
San Francisco *14, 25, 67, 71,
  72, 117, 131, 141, 144, 144*

San Francisco Chronicle 94
San Francisco Examiner 67
sandals *18, 42, 46, 46, 87*
Santa Monica *42, 58*
Schiaparelli, Elsa *77*
Sears *133*
Shakur, Tupac *140, 141*
shopping malls *135, 135*
shorts *56, 58, 58, 120, 124*
skateboards *10, 74, 80, 81,
  142, 150*
skiwear *74, 81*
Smith, Will *31*
snowboarding *80, 81*
sportswear *13, 25, 40, 64*
Strauss, Levi *100, 102*
sunglasses *110, 114*
Sunset magazine *45, 68*
surf culture *10, 11, 32, 38, 52,
  53,056, 56, 58*
swimsuits *10, 25, 32, 38, 40,
  45, 48, 49, 51, 58, 63*

Tabak of California *25, 152*
Tompkins Buell, Susie *141*
True Romance 110
tunic *127*
Turk, N. *93*
turtlenecks *147*

Valley Girl 135
Valley Girls *09*
Vertigo 116
Vogue 12, *49*

Weaver, Sylva *90, 137*
West Oakland *16*
Westernwear *87, 87, 94,
  97, 104*
Wild One, The 106, *106*
Williams, Carl *140*
Wilshire Boulevard *126, 131*
Wilson, Flip *32*
Wizard of Oz, The 28, *29*
Women's Wear Daily 31,
  58, 74
workwear *67, 87*
Wrangler *105*

Index

CREDITS

The publishers would like to thank the following sources for their kind permission to reproduce the pictures in this book.

Bob Stone/Conde Nast via Getty Images 8; /The Jay T. Last Collection of Graphic Arts and Social History Huntington Digital Library 10; /Tom Kelley/Getty Images 11; /Karen Radkai/Conde Nast via Getty Images 12; /Genevieve Naylor/Corbis via Getty Images 13; /San Francisco Historical Photograph Collection 15, 17; /© Joe Ramos 18; / UCLA 19; /Author collection 20; /University of California, The Bancroft Library 21; /Dick Whittington Studio/Corbis via Getty Images 23; / Fox Historic Costume Collection 24; / Photographs, Huntington Digital Library 26; /Pictorial Press/Alamy Stock Photo 27; /TCD/Prod.DB/Alamy Stock Photo 28; / Landmark Media/Alamy Stock Photo 29; / Moviestore Collection/Shutterstock 30; /THA/Shutterstock 32-33; /UCLA 34; / Harry Langdon/Getty Images 35; /Slim Aarons/Hulton Archive/Getty Images 39; /UCLA 40-41; /Author collection 43; / adsR/Alamy Stock Photo 44; /Neil Baylis/ Alamy Stock Photo 47; /Clifford Coffin/ Condé Nast via Getty Images 49; /© The Museum at FIT 50; /Photographs, Huntington Digital Library 51; / UCLA 52; / Tom Kelley/Getty Images 54-55; /Michael Ochs Archives/Getty Images 57; /George Long /Sports Illustrated via Getty Images/ Getty Images 59; /Eastman Originals Collection 62; /UCLA 65; /San Francisco examiner photograph archive, © The Regents of the University of California, The Bancroft Library, University of California, Berkeley 66; /Andy Hayt / Sports Illustrated via Getty Images/ Getty Images 69; / Camerique/Getty Images 70; /San Francisco Historical Photograph Collection 73; / Special Collections, J. Willard Marriott Library, University 74-75; /Bob Stone/Conde Nast via Getty Images 76; /Margaret Herrick Library, the Academy Foundation 78; / Author Collection 79; /Will Russell/ Getty Images 81; /Special Collections, J. Willard Marriott Library, University of Utah 85; /UCLA 86; /Author collection 88; /Slim Aarons/Getty Images 90-91; / Author collection 92-93; /Photographs, Huntington Digital Library 95; /Tom Kelley/Getty Images 96; /National Cowboy and Western Heritage Museum 97; / Author collection 98; /Special Collections && Archives, UC San Diego 101; /adsR/Alamy Stock Photo 102-103; /FlixPix/AlamyStockPhoto 104; / PictureLux/The Hollywood Archive 107; /Entertainment Pictures/Alamy Stock Photo 111; /CA girl from New School Archives 112; /UCLA 113; /Multimedia Archives, Special Collections, J. Willard Marriott Library, University of Utah 114; / Pictorial Press/Alamy Stock Photo 116; / THA/Shutterstock 118-119; /UCLA 121; / Bob Riha, Jr./Getty Images 122-123; /Jim Heimann Collection/Getty Images 125; / UCLA 127; /adsR/Alamy Stock Photo 129; /Author collection 130; /Los Angeles Public Library 133; /Everett Collection Inc/Alamy Stock Photo 134; /Margaret Herrick Library, the Academy Foundation 136-137; /Zuma Press, Inc./Alamy Stock Photo 140; /UCLA 142; /WENN Rights/ Alamy Stock Photo 143; /Bloomington, University Archives 144; /Barbara Alper/ Getty Images 145; /Art Frisch/The San Francisco Chronicle via Getty Images 146; /Album/Alamy Stock Photo 148; /AJ Pics/ Alamy Stock Photo 149; /Owen Harvey 151; /Author collection 152.